The Inner Life of Baby Doe Tabor

The Inner Life
of Baby Doe Tabor

Diane Brotemarkle

Photo credits:
Cover: Upper left, "Belle of Oshkosh," Oshkosh Public Museum, Oshkosh WI; Center, "Silver Queen of the West," in her royal ermine, Denver Public Library, Denver, CO (see also page 19); Lower right, Baby Doe the crone, Denver Public Library Western History Department, Denver, CO (see also page 63). Used with permission.

Cover background pattern is reprinted with permission from Anna Griffin, Inc.

All other images, personal collection, Diane Brotemarkle.

Electronic prepress: Gail Blinde, Fort Collins, CO

Library of Congress Cataloguing-in-Publication data
(LCCN) 2013913548

ISBN 978-0-9712372-2-3

dbrotemar@aol.com

Table of Contents

So much has been written about Elizabeth McCourt Doe Tabor, known as Baby Doe, that readers are most certainly entitled to inquire what more there can be to say. In this brief account, I focus on how her Catholicism and her devout nature might transform or at least modify the legends surrounding her—those dramatic ups and downs which have made her such a fascinating figure in the history of the American West. This task justifies a supplement to her story rather than another biography, and I invite the reader to so regard this monograph.

Hence, the reader will find selected biographical material rather than a life story, material that elaborates themes in her life especially enlightening in terms of her inner life, her spirituality, her psychology. When any of us thinks of a life story, we may usefully begin by proposing three questions: What were the circumstances of birth, all the givens of ancestry, gender, social status, historical period, location, all the features of our environment during our formative years? Next, we may seek to ascertain how these givens influenced our prime of life years measured as a series of successes and failures. Finally, how is a person's life history understood as a process of dying—of detaching from the world, of the growth and atrophy of the spirit? It will, of course, be left to our survivors to describe our stories in their entirety and objectivity.

The ancient Greeks, I am told, had over twenty words to express ideas of fate. One set of those words was personified as three mythological figures, women weavers, literally named the Fates, and their functions correspond to the questions I have just submitted. Clotho initiates the life tapestry, Lachesis feeds the individual threads into a pattern, and Atropos cuts the threads to complete the picture in all its details. Thus, the idea of fate as conceived herein involves life's givens, the hand that is dealt us, as well as how we play it. Fate as determinism is not our working definition here. Even as the Greeks had concepts of fate as destiny, as pre-destination, they also expressed, in the Classical period, the profound wisdom that "Character is Fate." The interplay of these forces, from without and within, constitutes, for me, the authentic story of Baby Doe Tabor. In the following pages I attempt to relate her life in terms of such dynamics as these. In the final analysis, one can never know another person's inmost spirituality, God's perspective, and I offer my supplement in a spirit of humility to all those who continue to find Lizzie Tabor, Baby Doe, fascinating.

Prologue

Winters are severe in Leadville, Colorado, in the mountainous and "magic" "Cloud City" nearly two miles above sea level. One wintry day in 1933, young Helen Skala stayed home from school because of a slight illness. In her monograph she recalls her father sitting by the window which looked out on Leadville's East 5th Street. Suddenly he exclaimed, "There is one of the most famous people in all of Colorado history. That is Baby Doe Tabor."

The snow lay deeply on the sidewalks and street where Mrs. Tabor trudged toward her errand in town, nearly a mile from her isolated cabin on Fryer Hill, next to the legendary Matchless mine. Helen recalled Mrs. Tabor's feet being wrapped in gunny sacking to keep them dry. Her father then told her the story of Lizzie Tabor's fairy-tale life, the story of Elizabeth McCourt Doe Tabor, who had become Colorado's Silver Queen, in control of immeasurable wealth—and then how she had lost everything: family, money, mansion, status, possessions.

Well, not quite everything.

She was 78 years of age that day in 1933 and still had two years on her lifespan. She was usually mentally alert although the following year would see her suffering from the onset of dementia. As she plowed through Leadville's East 5th Street that winter's day in 1933, she harbored a large share of remarkable memories—knowledge of the saints and sinners of Colorado's political scene, bitter and sweet nostalgia. It was always a surprise when a long-lost celebrity status resurrected itself in these, her waning years. Yet so it did. Baby Doe, who had once been internationally renowned for her wealth and beauty, now clung to a humble shoelace knotted as a rosary and still had a life of recompense and prayer.

Clotho: Circumstances of Birth

September 26, 1854, marked the birth of Lizzie McCourt, the fifth child of Elizabeth and Peter McCourt Sr. On October 7, 1854, she was christened (named for her mother) in the local St. Peter's Catholic parish: Elizabeth Nellis McCourt. Soon, she took on the middle name of a renowned local missionary priest, the Jesuit Father Bonduel, who achieved fame for his service to the Menominee tribe.[1] Because of her family's friendship with Fr. Bonduel, Lizzie became Elizabeth Bonduel McCourt. She was welcomed into this devout Irish-Catholic, middle-class, Victorian family in the recently incorporated (1853) near-frontier town of Oshkosh, Wisconsin. In the years that followed 1854, nine more children were born to the McCourts. None of the eleven-of-fourteen who survived, however, would achieve the American dream so spectacularly as "Baby" McCourt, destined to become a renowned beauty queen, destined to win the heart and fortunes of a Colorado silver bonanza king, H.A.W. (Horace) Tabor.

Among the most decisive facts about the circumstances of her birth is that she was born to become exceptionally beautiful. Her parents nicknamed her "Peaches," and the community dubbed her the "Belle of Oshkosh." As an adult, she was five feet two inches at full height and had long, lush strawberry blond hair that tumbled down her back below her waist on rare occasions when she did not wear it up. One of her biographers, John Burke, represents most writers about her as he praises her allurements: ". . . she had curly golden hair and eyes bluer than Lake Winnebago on a sunny afternoon, a tip-tilted nose, a rosebud mouth, a gardenia-pearl complexion. . . . She [also] had her share of Irish wit and of Irish willfulness."[2] Less apparent was the sense of power she experienced as invariably, wherever she went, heads turned. Celtic miners in Colorado, who saw her walking the streets of Central City, gaped: "Who's the fairy?" When Horace Tabor saw her descending the stairs in the Leadville hotel he owned, The Tabor Grand, he said to his attorney companion, Bill Hammett, "Isn't she the loveliest thing you ever saw?" Women usually resented these attentions from their menfolk, but only a woman who has experienced such power truly understands it.

Family values influenced her all her life, her birth family and the family she mothered. Her father, Peter McCourt Sr., was a clothier and tailor by trade. He owned and operated, with partners, a clothing emporium on Oshkosh's Main Street, a business destroyed three times by a series of four fires which devastated Oshkosh businesses, homes, and citizenry. But whether Lizzie's father worked out of his home or from the store, he served the fashion needs of his neighbors and was always a solid citizen during good times and bad. He and his wife Elizabeth instigated Lizzie's love of fashion and costuming, of modeling, and interest in fashion design. Lizzie Tabor, as a wealthy wife in the 1880s, was invariably remembered by Denver citizens not only for her beauty, money and good luck, but for her flamboyance, flair and style. (Many women disliked her precisely for these qualities.) As numerous photos of Baby Doe illustrate, she enjoyed pose and clothes. During her affluent years as Horace's wife, she designed uniforms for a local Guard, a 19th century version of a neighborhood watch and fire crew. She enjoyed needlework and personally monogrammed Horace Tabor's shirts and handkerchiefs. For herself, original Paris designs could be purchased. And, for her two daughters, then up-to-date clothing made of rare, expensive materials such as bejeweled imported silk and lace. In the years when she was no longer wealthy but still had the two girls to raise, Lizzie used her tailoring skills to make over the priceless Parisian gowns into party clothes for Lillie and Silver. In this way, her family's livelihood helped form her interests, skills, and values into her adult years.

Another force, one of nature, illustrated the "boom and bust" cycles of frontier life and left an indelible impression on Lizzie.

In the case of the McCourt family fortunes, the "bust" aspect of frontier fate was often the result of massive fires fed by the lumber mills of Oshkosh, appropriately nicknamed "sawdust city." It is no simple thing for a historian to represent an idea of such fires as forming the consciousness of Western American frontier citizens. That consciousness is revealed by eye-witnesses who reported one of 1875. The anonymous authors of an 1880s *History of the City of Oshkosh* considered a local newspaper article from the *Oshkosh Northwestern* worth reprinting. This vivid account helps us grasp the horrors induced by wildfires.

__The Beginning:__ It was about one o'clock P.M., and while the wind had reached its greatest fury, the startling whistles screamed out the alarm of fire along the line of mills and steam factories. It was a fearful day, and ten thousand souls started in wild excitement as they heard those first peals of the alarm whistles and well they might. The deep volumes of smoke, thick and black, that rolled up from Morgan's mill, showed too plainly what danger might be expected. Hardly had the great crowd gathered from all directions, when the spreading flames were already coiling and winding around the huge lumber piles that lay adjoining the mill. The wind was too strong, and the volume of flame too sudden for effective operation on the part of anybody. Great chunks of burning cinders came floating over into the lumber piles more adjacent to Main street, and they quickly caught. A fierce fight was waged among these piles, but the cinders became too numerous, and the ignitions too frequent to be baffled. The wind was blowing from the south-west. On came the rushing tide of flame, more furious than the descending flood of Mill River. The steamers seemed powerless to check such a fearless adversary. No sooner could they get set at work, than the enemy would charge with bayonets of fire, and drive them from their work.

It soon became apparent that it would sweep everything before it and the merchants on Main street began to more seriously consider the situation. In less than twenty minutes the fire had swept from Morgan's mill to the Milwaukee and St. Paul depot and freight house, and they were swept away like leaves in a blast furnace. The fire ripped through the planning, sash and blind mill of Lines, Libbey & Co, leaped to the sash, door and blind factory of Geo. Williamson & Co, taking the mill and yard of James & Stille in its course, and swept down to the planning mills of Bell and Rogers and Ben Henze, on Market street. In the meantime it had veered to the northward, up Light street to High, taking the Northwestern House and the large frame building opposite. The grocery store of W.H. Vallou, corner of Light and High streets, caught fire, and the flames swept along eastward, demolishing the handsome brick residence of J.C. Spalding, corner of High and Broad streets.

The Fire Reaches Main Street. *Thompson & Sprague's livery stable finally caught fire, and being a large wooden structure filled with hay and combustible matter, served to scatter fire all over the buildings on the west side of Main street. The first point of contact of Main street was in Wright's wooden block, next to S.M. Hay's brick building, and directly to leeward of the Livery stable. From the building the flames traveled with terrible swiftness in each direction, burning up toward The Northwestern on the north and spreading to the row of wooden building south from Hay and Bro's store.*

The Sight on Main Street. *When the flames swept over Main street, the sight on that and on adjoining streets beggars description. For a time those having stores and business places along Main street had great hopes that the fire would bear to the river. . . . When at length there was no doubt [that the fire would demolish the town] there was no time to be lost. Everything was in the wildest confusion. There was running to and fro in hot haste. Teams were eagerly sought for, empty vehicles were ravenously seized, and the sacking of those beautiful stores, and the piling of goods promiscuously into wagons, carts, or any available convenience, commenced in great earnest. The clerks of R.L. Bigger's had the omnibuses employed in removing their* *goods, and every available truck was engaged by the dry goods interests in that vicinity, to remove the goods to a place of safety. But, in spite of their untiring efforts, the dry goods men suffered large losses. The smoke became blinding, and the strife along Main street was terrible. Unbridled horses let loose from the livery stables came tearing by, while the yelling and screaming from man to man became perfectly terrifying. It was a wild scene which pen cannot picture.*

The article goes on describe the destruction of the post office which in turn fueled the flames that destroyed the Harding opera house and a Masonic Temple of Honor. The block containing the city offices was saved by the heroic efforts of nearly 50 men in a bucket brigade. A neighborhood of fashionable houses went up in flames as did the Presbyterian church, the German church, the Adams House as "the fire kept on its furious raid unchecked until it reached Bowen street, where it turned northward and on Waugoo street went a block beyond."

Bird's Eye View: A view of the great conflagration from the top of a tall building presented a romantic, yet an awful picture. Standing to the northward of the fire, on Main street, the scene was grand in the extreme. The whole area of the burnt district was burning at the same time. The buildings west of Main street had not yet burned down, while the flames had already spread far to the eastward, and the whole surface of the scene was one lurid glare of writhing, twisting, mocking flames. To the west, the further buildings were mostly gone, while the tall walls along Main stood for a moment tottering and swaying, then fell with a terrible roar and crash. Far to the eastward the house tops seemed but the playground of a thousand dancing demons reveling in the dire destruction of the hour. The steeple of the German church on Otter street, and the dome of the Adams House, shone up amidst the blackness of the upper smoke, glowing in columns of solid crimson, like the faint flickering of the setting sun through a dark storm cloud.

Small dwellings afar to the eastward, looked like so many bonfires in some exciting celebration, while men, women, and children, away down beneath, looked like pigmies in frantic gesture, hastening to and fro. The scene was wild, awful, and grand. Chaos ruled monarch of the hour, and man was dumb with awe.

After the Battle: *Night came on, and as darkness stole gradually upon the footsteps of the retreating sun, the scene changed. Excitement and anxious fear gave way to quiet despair and resignation. Tired humanity, relaxed and weary, began to seek a rest and refuge from the toils and fatigues of that awful day. Woe-begone and half discouraged, the outcast and hopeless began to gather their little store about them and seek a place of shelter from the raw night air. Where the hundreds went to, and where they found a roof to shelter them is a mystery. Even before the fire, house room was scarce, but now it seemed almost an impossibility to find it. But the unpleasantness of the circumstances was relieved in a measure, by the kindness and sympathy of those who were among the more fortunate. All who had a corner of room freely offered it to the sufferers.*

View by Night: *The view of the city by night from a distance was picturesque. The night itself was fearfully dark, and the red reflection from the ruins lit up the hazy atmosphere with a soft radiance, making a most beautiful sight. The thin smoke curling up from the heated mass of brick and mortar looked like incense burning upon some nightly altar. The long line of light, half vivid and half smothered in the darkness, gave a distinct outline of the burnt district. The tall, black buildings still remaining loomed up in perfect outline upon the light beyond like dark and solemn specters upon a moonlit sea. The ruin was over. Destruction had wrought its work, and the great day died like a Dolphin.*[3]

There were human casualties as several people died in the flames, either trapped by them alone or in the process of attempting to save others. More than 400 businesses were destroyed, and the valuation of damages exceeded two million dollars (approximately $50,000,000 by today's standards). A portion of the list of businesses destroyed reads: "Clothiers and tailors—McCourt & Cameron." And in a biographical note, the early *History of the City of Oshkosh* tells us: "The [most] prominent among the business men of that time was Peter McCourt, one of the most stirring and enterprising men of the place, and very popular. He was one of the leaders in the business enterprises of the early days of Oshkosh and a devoted friend to the interests of the city. He was eminently successful for many years but suffered heavily from a series of fires which seriously crippled his resources."[4]

Lizzie never forgot those fires. Even in the last decade of her life, she would describe them to interviewers like Caroline Bancroft, news reporters, and new acquaintances. The vivid description above serves to remind us that Oshkosh, Lizzie's girlhood home, was still a frontier town. Early histories of Oshkosh relate that, time after time, the town recovered from these disasters, rising "phoenix-like" out of the ashes. Lizzie took these community responses to heart. Thus, the series of fires (four of six total) occurred in 1859, May 1866, May 1874, July 1874 and wiped out her family financially. She learned the tensions and anxieties that accompany poverty. Too, they familiarized her with the "boom and bust" cycles typical of pioneering communities and taught her to adjust from prosperity to adversity, a process she would be required to repeat throughout her lifetime. It also taught her never to give up although Lady Luck has ceased to smile. She learned that when a family or a community pulls together, disasters can be overcome. Her experiences in this vein, together with her natural Irish optimism, lent her the strength in later years to carry on despite serious setbacks and reversals of fortune.

Although learning to cope with disaster was an aspect of Elizabeth Bonduel McCourt's formative years, her memories of youth were primarily good ones. When Caroline Bancroft visited with her in the late 1920s, Lizzie told Caroline that parties, dancing, boating, yachting, skating, theatricals and flirting were what she remembered most about growing up in Oshkosh. She kept scrapbooks about her beaux and wrote poetry of the Roses are Red/Violets are Blue variety. Her flirtatiousness earned her another name, "Baby," as her older brother James observed these games and connected them to a type of female, a "Babe," a naively coy girl. She enjoyed this affectionate compliment and retained her "Baby" nickname when she was no longer Baby McCourt but a married woman, Baby Doe.

She adored her family and worked (not always successfully) to maintain peaceable relationships with her younger brothers Peter, Phil, Stephen, John, Martin, Mark, and her baby sister Claudia, to whom she became virtually a second mother. The older siblings, Maggie, Tilly, Nealie and James were also dear to her.

Her girlhood in Oshkosh is undocumented, but she certainly had benefited from formal education. Most likely, she attended a Catholic school connected to St. Peter's. The city directory of 1868 relates that "this [church] has a school connected with it under the management of the Sisters of St. Dominic." In another source at the Oshkosh Public Library, 100 scholars are mentioned. Given her father's active role in St. Peter's, it seems likely he sent his children to this school, whose nuns would have taught her how to be a lady. Her posture was always ramrod straight, her carriage and manners exceptionally graceful. Her hands were soft (her parents did not allow Peaches to do laundry), never chafed, and well cared for all her life. She had elocution lessons which led the rough miners of Gilpin and Clear Creek counties in Colorado to describe her speech as "high falutin." She had also acquired clerical skills and was good at arithmetic. When Tabor gave her some oversight over the Tabor Grand Opera House in the mid 1880s, she had the skills to assist with accounting. She was, however, a paradox, a mischievous sprite. As Mrs. Horace Tabor, her servants called her a "regular roustabout" because she took on household tasks at will instead of waiting for the ministrations of servants. We get a glimpse here of the ordinary Lizzie McCourt as opposed to her image as Colorado's Silver Queen, a pose which also came naturally to her.

Her parents Elizabeth and Peter McCourt Sr. loved theater and passed this passion on to several of their offspring. Theater was more than just a hobby. An extended McCourt family was involved in the business. They established "McCourt Hall," where amateur entertainment was offered. McCourt Hall occupied the second floor above the clothing and tailoring shop. It was a successor to an earlier theater named Marks Hall, after the Chicago clothing merchants, the Marks Brothers, who had financed and founded Peter McCourt's clothing business in Oshkosh.

The Oshkosh Public Library contains a handwritten list of events in 1868 and 1869 when Lizzie was then fourteen years old. From advertisements in the local newspaper, we learn that Major

General Gibbon "of the famed Iron Brigade" was a speaker on December 23, 1868; Dr. Hayes lectured later the same month; on August 8, 1869, a Saturday, a troupe of four minstrels combined into one, were scheduled to give two performances the following Tuesday and Wednesday evenings; later that August McCourt Hall hosted a Republican rally. In February and March, 1869, there were grand balls. On January 23, Miss Olive Logan "talks on Paris—City of Luxury." And so forth, with several theatricals mentioned. The Democratic party held its district convention there. Churches of many denominations sponsored events and local clubs held meetings. And, until St. Peter's parish church was completed, the McCourt family moved services from their home into the public space of McCourt Hall. Lizzie's youthful experiences thus introduced her to many aspects of the wider world beyond Oshkosh and accounts for a level of sophistication she exhibited all her life.

Mr. Charles Nevitt, who had moved to Oshkosh in August of 1874, bestowed a personal collection of photos, scrapbooks, and autobiographical material upon the Oshkosh Museum, and among the papers there is a description of what it was like to be among the McCourt theater enthusiasts:

> During the years from 1875 to 1879 I took part in many theatrical performances in the opera house for the benefit of the Catholic Church. The leading spirit in these enterprises was Mrs. James McCourt, known on the American stage as Amelia Watts. She had always been a protestant, but upon marrying handsome James McCourt, "Jim," as everyone called him, she joined the Catholic Church. She was a leader in the church choir and of course had a role in all plays, I playing opposite. We

played "Meg's Diversion," "Lady Audley's Secret," "Nan, the Good-for-Nothing" and other plays. Peter McCourt and Mrs. Andrew Haben [Lizzie's older sister Tillie], brother and sister of Baby Doe. . . also had parts in the plays. We made a lot of money for the Church and the priest, Father O'Malley, was grateful.[5]

The family had connections with professional actors as well as amateurs. James, the eldest of the McCourt offspring, married Dollie Biddel, who went on to achieve a national reputation as the actress Amelia Watts. At the height of her career, she appeared onstage with Edwin Booth, a leading actor of the times. She later remarried, becoming in her private life, Mrs. Henry Pratt.

Others among Lizzie's relatives made successful careers in America's stage and movie industry. According to a letter Claudia McCourt's son Bob McCabe of Chicago wrote to Leadville historian Edward Blair:

> . . . I had hoped to mention [in previous correspondence] our English connection. One of Elizabeth Tabor's sisters [Margaret] married an Englishman name of Courtney, and had two children, Maud and George, both actors. Maud married Finlay Currie who, among other acting and movie parts, played Magwitch in [a 1935 production of Charles Dickens' novel] Great Expectations.[6]

Twenty years after her adventures in McCourt Hall, Lizzie acted as secretary of her husband's Tabor Entertainment Company, (formed 1892) and scheduled theatricals from important New York, London, and Eastern U.S. theatrical companies. They came West to play for the Silver Circuit, as the Rocky Mountain theater business was known. These Silver Circuit shows called upon the best names of the times: Sarah Bernhardt, Helen Modjeska, Emma Abbot, Edwin Booth and others. Tabor's opera houses in Leadville and Denver were indeed "Grand," providing a first-class venue for the actors, playwrights, and production people in the American theater of the Gilded Age. When stars of the stage came to Denver, Lizzie assisted her manager brother Peter, held receptions, solved problems, provided for housing personnel and even, perhaps, for the difficult hauling of props and costumes by train up the steep Rocky Mountains to Leadville, or off to Aspen, Pueblo and other stops on the Circuit. When the show in Denver was over, the female lead would be presented a huge bouquet of Lizzie's favorite calla lilies. She enjoyed the productions themselves from her place in Box A, and although some of Denver's society women resented her "queening it" in Box A, Lizzie had contributed significantly to the cultural life of the fledgling city of Denver. When the same society women requested the use of the Tabor Grand for charitable events, they had to swallow their pride and call upon Mrs. Tabor. Admittedly, she sometimes dreamed of vengeance upon her female enemies, but at last she agreed because she could never resist helping for a charitable cause.

In this way, the McCourt family devotion to theater, blessed by Tabor money, accounts for top-flight entertainment flourishing in early Denver. It also explains Lizzie's encouragement of her daughter Silver's interest in acting. A bit of early film trivia concerning the Tabor family was set in southern Colorado. Lizzie and Horace's daughter Silver played a bit part for one of the rare pre-Hollywood film companies, one operating in Colorado Springs in 1915. Evidence suggests that their operation may have been in violation of Edison's patent on moving picture cameras, but here was a pioneering if short-lived enterprise. Silver had a lisp which prevented her from assuming speaking parts or major roles. Her sultry, brunette beauty is captured in a publicity photo related to the production.

Lizzie's days of wine and roses would pass as would her aspirations for a stage career; her husband would die and her daughters disappoint her expectations as would her mining claims. Her Catholic spirituality, however, abided. The McCourt family was devoutly Roman Catholic, a fact which should not be taken lightly for anyone interested in Baby Doe Tabor. Her religion was more than an "influence." It was a prime motivation for her actions and a determining factor in her self-assessments. Her middle name, Bonduel, carried meaning for her in later years, for she was devoted to fathers of the Jesuit Society, and, indeed, priests represented earthly saints for her. As a recluse, she never turned away from a Catholic friend. Her father had come to Canada as a two-year old, during the first of the devastating potato famines, making Lizzie a second-generation Irish American. Having emigrated to America, Peter McCourt prospered in Oshkosh, but the family remembered the poverty that often accompanied the uprooted Irish, a people who had little to transport except their Christian faith. Despite the fact that Lizzie sometimes broke the rules of her Catholic upbringing—a fact the newspapers used to their financial advantage—she never abandoned her habits of prayer. She remained a devout personality, as all who knew her would attest. In the midst of great loss and tribulation, she found consolation and inspiration in "the Faith."

Growing up in a household of numerous siblings and an affectionate, warm family atmosphere, Lizzie consistently placed the highest priority upon family, even when she felt compelled to choose between family and religious commandments. That is, she violated the prescribed rules of the Roman Catholic Church and broke several of the Ten Commandments when by doing so she could benefit her Oshkosh family and found a family of her own with Horace Tabor. Perhaps it is a bit too easy for those sitting on the sideline of her life to point to the hypocrisy involved.

She was, as well, a product of the Victorian era. It shaped her sense of propriety and her despair when she violated those standards. Focusing as it did on death, Victorian America gave rise to the phenomenon known as Spiritualism. Across the Fox River from Oshkosh, in the small community of Omro, Wisconsin, another theater was being held, for Omro was one of the first sites of Spiritualist activities in the 1850s when the movement (it had begun in upstate New York) began to accelerate. Spiritualism was the rage during Lizzie's growing up years, and she had, as it were, a front row seat from which to observe the excitement. The ideas and goals of the Spiritualists would influence her in later years as family members passed on and Lizzie considered the opportunities to communicate with loved ones a possibility not to be ignored.

In summary, during her years in Oshkosh, Lizzie learned a lasting love of the theater, a profound sense of familial duty to help and support one another, and an abiding commitment to Roman Catholicism. She was deeply identified by her Irish-American ethnic roots as well as her upbringing as a proper Victorian woman who strained at the boundaries of that identity, especially as a progressive-minded and ambitious businesswoman. As a young woman, "she possessed a natural vitality, strong constitution, charm and astuteness—but also flirtatiousness and vanity."[7] Her strong back, she later claimed, was a gift from God because she was destined to bear a heavy burden of tribulations. Her health had been nearly perfect, except for an occasional cold and neuralgia headaches. These perhaps contributed to her reclusiveness and may have caused the "cure," laudanum, to incite vivid dreams, which she recorded, among others, in notes and on calendars as long as she lived.

In addition, Caroline Bancroft states that she ". . . loved mystery and romance. She cloaked her life in subterfuge and pretensions, the better to adapt reality to her American notions."[8] Whatever 'American notions' may have contributed to her secrecy and subterfuge, we do know that privacy was vital to her. She had developed a code in which to disguise written communications between her husband and herself. While this could have been quite common among wealthy business people of the time, we may question whether subterfuges provide evidence of deeper disturbances in her personality. John Burke, in his biography of Baby Doe remarks that all the attention she received (being a 'pocket Venus') naturally resulted in some narcissistic traits.[9] The comment is almost dismissive, since her remarkable beauty did indeed cause a stir wherever she went. In the last section of this work, I consider the question of whether narcissism might be more for her than an environmentally induced state, stemming from male attention. Perhaps nature—or what we today would call DNA—programmed some borderline "paranoia" into her history. If so, her inner life should be regarded in a very different way than has so far been published.

Her physical attributes, social interests, and moral characteristics thus being established in her growing-up years, she was prepared to marry and she wanted to marry well. Her choice fell upon the well-to-do Harvey Doe, son of William H. Doe, a prominent man of Oshkosh. At age 22, she was married in St. Peter's church to the protestant Harvey Doe. The church was over-flowing with witnesses to the wedding.

Her father-in-law owned promising mining claims in the state of Colorado, then, in 1876, newly established in statehood. The newlyweds spent their wedding night on a train bound for Denver. Lizzie McCourt Doe had stars in her eyes as she gazed upon her adoring husband, confident that the mining claims which were the Doe family wedding gift, would yield easy wealth. The world was her oyster, indeed. The pot of gold at the end of the rainbow was within reach.

However, her marriage to Harvey Doe was stormy and brief. After three years the divorce was final, but the marriage was troubled almost from the start. After six months, her mother-in-law, Elizabeth Doe, moved to Central City from Oshkosh with the four daughters. She had never welcomed "that fast Baby McCourt" into her family, and now Lizzie was subjected to relentless criticism. When she realized that Harvey was not going to defend her against these attacks, she contemptuously dismissed him as "that Mama's boy." When she realized that Harvey was no longer interested in working the Fourth of July mine, she hurled a piece of ore at him, narrowly missing his head. When the Doe's moved to Denver as William H. was elected to the House of Representatives from Clear Creek County, Harvey played about town, effectively deserting his young wife and their unborn son.[10]

Meanwhile, Lizzie had come under the protection of Central City's dashing bachelor, Jake Sands (Sandelowsky at birth). Like her parents, he hailed from Ithaca, New York, and like them owned a clothing emporium. Lizzie's background meant that she could offer Jake competent assistance in the store, Pelton & Sands. He liked to dance as did Lizzie. When they showed up together at a lowlife bar called the Shoe Fly for a dance, Harvey failed to attend, and questions about Mrs. Doe's reputation were quietly discussed. When her son was born, it was Jake, not Harvey, who summoned the midwife. The child did not survive the day of his birth, and Lizzie went into mourning. Although it seemed Jake would marry her once a divorce was obtained, Lizzie wrote in her scrapbook, "Baby is frightened." This brief phrase could serve as the mantra of her whole life. She was reluctant to return home, since her family, devastated by the fires, were in great financial straits and had several young ones still to care for. Heartsick and guilt-ridden, she agreed to accompany Jake to Leadville where he could open a second clothing store in the elegant Tabor Grand Opera's ground floor.

Once in Leadville, booked into the Clarendon Hotel, Lizzie drew the attention of the Silver King Horace Tabor. Shortly thereafter, Lizzie was a "kept" woman and Jake Sands had been paid $5000 to cover his gifts to Lizzie and renounce his claim. Decades later, Denver's only woman attorney, Mary Lathrop, who knew the aging Baby Doe, stated that this bandying about of Baby Doe from one man to the next accounted in some degree for her late-life reclusiveness.[11] However, Carolyn Bancroft's widely read "biography" characterized Lizzie not as a victim but as an assertive and calculating flirt who achieved her role as Horace's wife with her cunning wiles. Although the latter impression clung to her legend, the former is probably closer to the truth. Bancroft fictionalized her Baby Doe as a "naughty lady" like most of the women she wrote about, a projection of Bancroft's own non-conformist persona. This was the end of her youth. Now, the fateful weaver Lachesis would represent the complexities of her prime of life.

Lachesis: Pattern of Life

What is the shape of sorrow? How does a writer give outline and texture to sin, grief, and ill fortune? What is the color of fun and even joy? Great painters know these are not unanswerable questions, but putting such into words is a different matter. Now we have to turn to the stories. rather than to the illustrative tapestries that replace a thousand words. For Baby Doe, her obsession with motherhood and her hero-worship of her husband, the stories ill suit a fairy-tale princess such as she was frequently described. To what extent, we ask, did her character determine the outcomes of her closest relationships in the nuclear family?

In a 1956 memoir entitled, *When Denver and I Were Young,* Edwina Fallis recalled Denver in the 1880s. One day when she was eight years old, she accompanied her aunt and grandmother on a shopping trip downtown. In front of McNamara's new department store on 16th and California, little Edwina saw an elaborate carriage lined with baby-blue satin.

"Oh, look, Grandma! That beautiful carriage. . . .Those horses! Ain't they pretty?"

"Don't say "ain't."

"That's Baby Doe's carriage," said Aunt Carrie. "Ma, she's probably in McNamara's store now. We'd better not go in, had we?"

"If I want anything in this store I'll not let that woman keep me out." Grandma put her nose in the air, lifted up her long skirts, and sailed through the door, straight up the main aisle to the stocking counter.

Aunt Carrie pretended not to see, but I saw and held back to get a better look at the beautiful golden-haired lady dressed in baby-blue satin to match the lining in her carriage. And what do you think she had in her arms? Her little baby in long clothes made of real lace.

The fancy dress was so long it hung down almost to the floor.

Some clerks stood around and I heard one of them say, "Will you please, Mrs. Tabor, show us little Lillie's bootees with the diamond buttons?"

The lovely lady smiled and pulled up the long dress and the white flannel petticoat. Aunt Carrie and I stood there, breathless, hoping to see the bootees too.

But Grandma called, "Carrie, come over here and tell me how many of these black lisle stockings you want. They are on sale, three pairs for a dollar."

So, I never got to see the bootees with the diamond buttons.

Grandma walked out the store the same way she had walked in, and I wondered why she lifted her skirt when she passed Baby Doe Tabor when she had let them drag over the filthy sidewalk.[12]

Denver Post writer Eva Hodges correctly headlined Baby Doe as "Admired. . . Despised." Often, children did the admiring while their elders did the despising, as is illustrated in an article in *Colorado Magazine* about the early theater in Denver. Eliza Logan Burt reported that when she was twelve, she often went to the Tabor Grand Opera in Denver because her family was in the business and entertained there. She says:

We saw the Tabors often. Father was a stern, puritanical man, and he forbade me to even look at Baby Doe. However, I often sneaked into the wings to gaze at her in the Tabor box—she was so dazzling to a small girl—then I would run for fear father would catch me there. Augusta used to come to the theatre and just stand outside, sometimes without even a hat, crying there alone, waiting to see Tabor enter the theatre. . . .[13]

Thus, Denver citizens shunned the second Mrs. Horace Tabor and pitied the first. As Caroline Bancroft noted, Lizzie was "déclassé." Envy of her youth, wealth, and beauty was no doubt a factor. Furthermore, the first Mrs. Tabor garnered great sympathy as she wept publicly and maintained to the court that she had sought the divorce "not willingly, not willingly." Many friends believed that if Baby Doe had not captured Tabor's affections, he and Augusta would have patched up their differences. For these and many other reasons, Lizzie was resented, even despised. Then, too, there was her status as a divorced Catholic among a Protestant and Victorian majority.

Horace's biographer Duane Smith rightly corrected one of these impressions (alas, after a century of percolating), that Lizzie was a home wrecker. Smith writes: "Nor was she the 'other woman' who broke up his first marriage. The ground work for that rift had been laid before she came on the scene."[14] Augusta refused to follow her husband into his new lifestyle as a wealthy mine owner, Colorado's "Silver King." If he insisted on a mansion, she wanted to continue taking in boarders and grazing a useful cow on the elegant lawn. According to another Tabor biographer, Lewis Gandy, Augusta was a "termagant," a nag. Still, Gandy was among this hardy pioneering woman's supporters, dubbing her "vinegary but good." Perhaps Augusta had wanted a divorce by late 1881. She changed her mind at some point, and sued for "separate maintenance," claiming that Horace had abandoned her and failed for two years to support her so that she had had to take in boarders. As John Burke points out, this was nonsense and most Coloradans knew it.[15] Not until January, 1883, was Augusta's settlement of at least a quarter of a million dollars agreed upon and Horace got the divorce he had long sought. However, it was Augusta, the tragic figure, that frightened wives and moved the hearts of Denver society. Lizzie was the interloper.

Not all the censure was undeserved. Lizzie's affair with Jake Sands had been grist for the gossip mills, for after her break-up with Harvey Doe it was widely known that she lived with a man (the Central City bachelor clothier Jake Sandelowsky) who was not her husband.[16] Once married, she and Horace might have lived down these resentments as they took up respectable lives, benefiting Denver with buildings, donations, and support of many charitable causes. However, a series of scandals published far and wide by the nation's newspapers in the spring of 1883 damaged their reputation beyond repair, setting them up for endless satire, eventually dooming Horace's political career and turning Baby Doe into an unsavory legendary figure. These four scandals may be designated by the order of their publication (not their chronology) as: 1) The Washington D.C. wedding; 2) The Durango divorce, and 3) The St. Louis wedding, and 4) the Bill Bush lawsuit. Of these, the first was the most damaging to Baby Doe personally, but not for the reasons the newspapers suggested. The victims of the first one, this wedding, were Lizzie's father, Peter McCourt Sr., and the officiating priest, Fr. Chapelle of St. Andrew's Parish, Baltimore, Maryland. Both men had their reputations tarnished. The story goes like this:

The Second Commandment: Just after 9 p.m., March 1, 1883, Lizzie McCourt Doe, aged 28, was joined in matrimony with Horace Tabor, who was 24 years her senior. At Washington D.C.'s Willard Hotel, the groom had ordered a lavish "perfect fairyland" of decoration, including roses, violets, camelias, and—Lizzie's favorite—calla lilies, symbolizing purity. Clever arrangements of flowers and vines represented shamrocks, wedding rings, and an arrow-pierced Cupid. The announcement became public the next day and claimed the affair was "the social sensation of the season." Furthermore, "Mrs. Tabor is considered the most charming and beautiful woman ever seen in Washington." The bride's white gown cost $7,500; the groom's gift was a $75,000 necklace, including the Isabella diamond, allegedly once the property of the 16th century Portugese queen.

The press release also emphasized the presence of the President, Chester Arthur, his attentiveness to the bride. However, Washington

The Second Commandment

"The second commandment states, 'Thou shalt not take the name of the Lord thy God in vain.'

We must speak with reverence of God and of the saints, and of all holy things, and must keep our lawful oaths and vows.

An oath is the calling upon God to witness the truth of what we say. It is permitted when it is ordered by lawful authority or is needed for God's honor or our own or our neighbor's good. What we swear to must be true.

A vow is a deliberate promise made to God to do something that is pleasing to Him. It must be a true promise, made to God with deliberation, and the thing promised must be good and possible.

Not to fulfill a vow is a sin, mortal or venial, according to the nature of the vow and the intention we had when making it. When a person enters a religious order, he or she takes the vows of poverty, chastity and obedience.

A vow should be given serious deliberation, and in important matters it is advisable to seek the confessor's advice before taking one.

The second commandment forbids all false, rash, unjust and unnecessary oaths, as well as blasphemy, cursing and profanity."

The owners of Baby Doe's cabin, the John K. Mullen family, recovered a newsclip in the cabin shortly after Baby Doe's death. Eventually this and other scraps were donated to the Tabor collection of the Colorado Historical Society. Her interest in this topic stems from the false testimony her family gave to allow the wedding to Horace Tabor in Washington, D.C., March, 1883. It also relates to a vow she made, espousing herself to God.

newspapers soon modified this picture generated by the groom's staff before the event. The President dropped in briefly, danced with the bride and left early. The diamond necklace had not arrived from Europe, so was not displayed. Shortly after the President left at 10:45, the festivities ended. The whole affair lasted under two hours.

This ceremony was made possible by Horace's Denver divorce from Augusta, which had been drawn out for months as Augusta's attorney dragged out the settlement process. It was facilitated as well by the bride's father in cooperation with Fr. Chapelle and the Bishop of Baltimore.

Lizzie McCourt's family from Oshkosh presented their own set of problems with the party atmosphere Horace had hoped to create. They were in the deep mourning period over the death of their son James the previous September, and celebrations were not yet timely according to Victorian mourning protocols. Horace complained that Lizzie's family, in their black garb, looked like a "flock of crows" as they watched the dancing from the sidelines. He had had to buy black onyx cufflinks especially on account of their status as mourners. Thus, the McCourts had compromised Victorian standards of respectability in order to support their beloved daughter. Yet, a far worse situation developed, one that required Lizzie's father to swear that his divorced daughter was in fact free to marry in the Catholic church. In other words, he agreed to violate the Second Commandment, "Thou shalt not take the name of the Lord Thy God in vain." On the Bible he had sworn "so help me God" that his daughter was free to marry in the Catholic church.

On the day following the ceremony, the officiating priest, Father Chapelle of Saint Andrew's parish, Baltimore, returned the fee for his services because he had been informed that Lizzie McCourt Doe was a divorcee and not free to marry in the Catholic Church since she had a living husband, Harvey Doe. The wedding had become a national media circus, and Father Chapelle was forced to admit to the press that he had been deceived as he had not known that *both parties were divorced persons* [Italics mine]. Lizzie's parents, he informed the reporters, had provided sworn testimony that she was free to marry. Thus, he had in good faith proceeded with the ceremony. Why would a lifelong devout Catholic such as Peter McCourt mislead a priest about his daughter's status? He explained this to his local newspaper, the Oshkosh *Northwestern* in the aftermath of the Washington wedding. The family had originally planned a private ceremony before a justice of the peace. However, they were informed that "according to the laws of the District of Columbia, no magistrate or public officer had authority to [perform the ceremony], the only legal person to which such power is granted in that district being a properly ordained minister or priest or a Quaker official." In view of this fact, the *Northwestern* comments, Mr. McCourt "was compelled to call upon a priest and did so by going to Father Chapelle who consented to the performing of a simple private ceremony."[17] Apparently, since the family had no connections to Quakers or Protestant ministers, a Catholic priest was the only option. To meet the requirements of the diocese, Peter McCourt had to affirm that his daughter was free to marry, and this he did, no doubt feeling the burden of this dilemma. Peter McCourt never recovered his self-respect because of this deception and on his deathbed shortly thereafter, expressed his shame and regret.

Meanwhile the reporters misunderstood Father Chapelle's claim that he did not know both parties were divorced. They interpreted this as though Father Chapelle did not know *either* party was divorced. Since Horace's divorce from Augusta had been front page news across the land, the idea that Father Chapelle did not know Horace was divorced was ludicrous. His good faith involvement in the wedding altogether was questioned, and among the indignant was Peter McCourt's pastor at St. Peter's in Oshkosh, Father James O'Malley. He had been approached by Oshkosh reporters soon after the national press coverage of the Washington wedding. Father O'Malley was asked by his friendly press how Father Chapelle could have been unaware of Horace's divorce, and the priest followed up with a letter of inquiry to the Baltimore priest. Heavy with sarcasm and unwilling to attempt to undo this complex can of worms, Fr. Chapelle replied, "My not answering your [letter] was not prompted by any feeling of disrespect, but I thought that the Oshkosh press having sent my statement of the affair throughout the country, the newspapers would give ample satisfaction to anxious inquirers like yourself."

Despite insinuations that the priest had lied about his understanding of Horace's status as a divorced person, such was not the case. Horace Tabor's marriage to Augusta had occurred in her family home officiated by a justice of the peace or a Unitarian minister. Since Horace had not been married to Augusta in a Catholic ceremony, or by an ordained Christian minister, he was considered free to marry under the Roman Catholic Church's canon law. Horace's marriage to Augusta was recognized as civilly valid but not as sacramental. The newspapers never claimed that Father

Chapelle was unaware that Horace had been previously married. Rather the news stories correctly stated that he was unaware that *both* parties were divorced. Because the reporters did not understand that Father Chapelle and his superiors would have looked at Horace's and Lizzie's marital histories as two separate cases, they did not accurately depict Father Chapelle's role. It was Lizzie who was not free to marry. The knowledge that Father Chapelle must have had about Horace's marital situation (including his status as a non-Catholic) was no deterrent to his official capacity at the Tabor wedding. Regarding Lizzie's status, the priest had the family's sworn testimony that she was free to marry. Furthermore, in any Catholic wedding, there were protocols to be observed, especially the public announcement of the upcoming wedding from the pulpit on three consecutive Sundays. This process, called the banns of marriage, was waived in the case of the Tabors. Thus, the McCourt family in Oshkosh says in the interview with the *Daily Northwestern* that the Baltimore bishop, Father Chapelle's superior, gave a "dispensation" so that the marriage could be solemnized. The news reporters' failure to distinguish between "either" and "both" vis a vis Lizzie and Horace's marital status perhaps cast Fr. Chapelle in an unwarranted scandalous position.

There seems to have been a rift between the Oshkosh McCourt family and their long-time friend and spiritual advisor, Fr. O'Malley. After this, they frequented St. Mary's parish instead of St. Peter's. Peter McCourt died within a year and never recovered his self-respect even though he had been rather cornered into his sanction of his daughter's Catholic marriage. Nothing in the vast literature about Baby Doe Tabor suggests that she was affected by any of this.

However, her devotion to her father and his sorrow over a mortal sin (a serious—damning if unrepented—offense against God) must have cast deep shadows of regret at the memory of her wedding. He had not had the peaceful, happy death he deserved and it was her doing. She would not have forgotten this in later years of repentance. Among the thousands of snippets from newspapers found among her effects after her death is one she clipped, probably from the *Denver Catholic Register.* It explains the nature and meaning of the Second Commandment including the giving of false testimony.

Three other newspaper scandals appeared subsequently, though they concerned events prior to March 1, 1883. The second account claimed that Horace had filed divorce papers on his own authority and without Augusta's knowledge in Durango, Colorado, in the summer of 1882. The courts eventually judged it invalid. More sympathy for Augusta resulted from such underhanded scheming. Only later would Colorado citizens learn that the phony divorce placed Horace in the role of bigamist. It required the story of the St. Louis wedding to bring this to light.

Thirdly, Horace Tabor, having business in St. Louis, Missouri, convinced a friend named Judge Dyer to perform a marriage ceremony between himself and Baby Doe. This late September affair in 1882 was to have been a secret. For six months it remained so. In late March, 1883, the Denver newspapers launched headlines. Sensational reports of Horace Tabor's "bigamy" filled the pages since his Durango divorce had been deemed invalid. On September 21, 1882, Lizzie's beloved older brother James McCourt had died suddenly of complications from a broken leg. She hastened to Oshkosh to be with her family. When the Oshkosh *Northwestern* newspaper heard of the latest scandal involving Baby Doe and Horace Tabor, they published an alternative theory denying Baby Doe's involvement.

A Northwestern reporter had wasted much time today in trying to find something that would throw some light on the matter, but has been unable to discover anything so far but what indicates that either the above report [the Tabor-McCourt secret marriage in St. Louis, Sept. 30, 1882] is a canard or else the time has been misstated. For it is the opinion of those who have the best chances for knowing that Miss McCourt was in this city on September 30th. James McCourt met with an accident which caused his death September 16, [1882]. Within two or three days thereafter telegrams were sent to the relatives and among others to his sister Lizzie in Denver, announcing his probable death. James died on the 21st and on the evening of the 23rd Lizzie arrived here. The funeral took place on the 24th and during the week following the family were all busy attending to matters pertaining to James' estate, and according to the statement of those familiar with the family, Lizzie remained here for two weeks after the funeral and was, therefore, in this city on Sept. 30. The same authority says with much positiveness that Peter McCourt, her father, has not been out of town since the funeral. . . .[18]

Because of a variant newspaper account, biographers have accepted the St. Louis marriage of September, 1882, as a fact of Baby's Doe's life. Unlike the responsible journalism of the *Oshkosh Daily Northwestern* the Colorado account of the St. Louis wedding is outright scandalmongering. Burke reports that the county clerk who discovered the paperwork alerted Augusta and that it was through her the scandal erupted. Torn between a desire to inflict harm on her ex-husband and to let it go, Augusta behaved like a loose cannon in Lizzie's life. However, three bits of evidence that Lizzie was not there support this view: 1) Oshkosh citizens bear witness that she was in Oshkosh; 2) Lizzie was grief-stricken over the loss of her favorite older sibling, and this would have been reason enough to postpone her wedding ceremony; 3) her signature does not appear on the matrimonial paperwork. These were Victorian times and the death of a near family member demanded certain signs of respect. Lizzie would not have waltzed off on a disreputable elopement under these circumstances.

On the other hand, Horace's friend, Judge Dyer, claimed that the bride had been there, and—whoever this was—she was the most beautiful woman he'd ever seen. Is this sufficient evidence to reject the *Oshkosh Northwestern's* denial? I find the above three testimonies decisive and I can only conclude that Judge Dyer was attesting to an event that had never happened and to seeing a woman he had never seen, because his friend Horace Tabor needed this testimony. Perhaps Horace created this record thinking that Lizzie might be pregnant and wanting to protect her with paperwork should that be the case. Certainly, neither Horace nor Judge Dyer thought the record would become public without their consent. Only by an accident did a Durango clerk come across the marriage record and publicize it. This stroke of bad luck snowballed into merciless satire on the part of Denver journalist Eugene Field, who jibed: "A feller should have the right to marry as many women as he wants as often as he wants!"

All this destroyed her already faltering reputation. Horace's wealth protected him from overt criticism among his associates, but privately former friends and supporters began to think of him as a fool. In yet a fourth scandal, Horace's long-time right-hand-man

Bill Bush sued Tabor for money he said Tabor owed him for being a point man in Tabor's efforts to divorce his wife and marry Baby Doe. Tabor defended himself and expressed his indignation that Bush's wife was among those who shunned his wife. He had paid Bush well for all kinds of services, including work managing the opera house, and deserved some loyalty. After all, Tabor said, his wife was "a nice lady." Bush's lawsuit didn't succeed, but more damage had been done. As usual, even though Horace won in the courts, as in the Bush case, he lost in the press and therefore in public opinion. Many people thought that Mrs. Bush's refusal to acknowledge Baby Doe was, like their own, based on sympathy for Augusta. However, the Bush's were Catholic, and it seems likely they also were offended by the deceptions Bill's employer and his bride had resorted to, including lying to a priest and engaging in a sham of a Catholic wedding.

In summary, the aftermath of Baby Doe's wedding to Horace included these consequences: Denver citizens poured out sympathy for Horace's ex-wife Augusta even though she had initiated the separation in the courts in a bid for "separate maintenance" before Horace had noticed Lizzie Doe. (He was said to have been accompanied on business trips with a few of Denver's soiled doves after Augusta instigated the separation and before he invited Baby Doe into his life.) After the wedding, Horace quickly made Lizzie his sole heir and executrix, thereby alienating Horace's grown son Maxcy. Horace's longstanding, close business relationship with Bill Bush was ruptured amid scandalous newspaper coverage. Horace's personal life was treated with derision in the press, led by "humorist" Eugene Field. Horace lost two bids for the governorship of Colorado, despite his huge donations to the state Republican party. His political career, once promising (he'd been touted for U.S. President in a New Jersey newspaper in 1883), failed. Horace restored the Oshkosh McCourt in-laws' fortunes with a gift of $200,000, but Peter McCourt Sr. left the parish he helped found—St. Peter's—and died guilt ridden shortly after—because he had sworn falsely about the freedom of his daughter to marry in the Church. Lizzie's brother Peter was brought in to manage the theater business, a factor in Bill Bush's alienation. The Tabor newlyweds, optimistic about Horace's political career that might well rise to obtaining the Presidency, underestimated the effects of bad press just as they failed to appreciate those of economic patterns in American life. The McCourt family had taught Lizzie how to be a devoted wife. This would turn out to be the deciding factor in her successful though scandal-ridden second marriage.

The wealthy Tabors eventually moved into a mansion on Sherman street; it sat upon a full city block. They retained at least five servants, and appeared in any one of three silk-lined carriages with splendid matched horses for each. Opulence marked their domestic arrangements: precious crystal and textiles from Europe, Parisian gowns, the finest hand-carved mahogany furniture from the best interior decorators. They purchased classical style statuary and displayed it on the front lawn. When puritanical citizens complained about the nakedness of them, Baby Doe bestowed draperies on her garden art. Such compromises with her detractors became the norm of her days. Women (even Colorado's First Lady) who scorned her publicly on Wednesday had to beg her permission on Thursday for their charity events to be held at the Tabor Grand Opera House.

Nor did household management under an unlimited budget compensate altogether for the social ostracism. Women like Edwina

Fallis' grandmother might drag her skirts on dirty sidewalks and lift them in disdain passing by Baby Doe Tabor to prove that money never, *never* bought respectability. That many Denver women committed sins of self-righteousness and envy regarding Mrs. Tabor was cold comfort. Drawing family around her was a way of circling the wagons. The playmate of her youth, brother Peter McCourt, came and was given management of the Opera House. Brother Phil also found employment as did her sister Nealie's (Cornelia McCourt Last) family, the John Last's. Augusta snidely observed to her friends that boatloads of McCourts were doubtless bound from Ireland to feed at the trough of her ex-husband. In fact, only three or four actually got on the payroll. Gradually, the press scandals subsided and Lizzie thought to enjoy the freedoms money could buy.

Among the buffers provided against her detractors were Catholic clergy and nuns. She enjoyed giving free tickets to Opera House shows to friends like her pastor at Sacred Heart in Denver, Fr. Guida, who was, like her childhood idol Fr. Bonduel, a Jesuit. She had originally attended the cathedral, Immaculate Heart parish, but her presence at Sunday mass created such a stir among parishioners that Bishop Machebeuf asked her to remove herself to the smaller parish, Sacred Heart. This appears to have worked out happily.[19]

Additional respite from Denver persecutors was provided as the Tabors made two trips to Europe. The renowned Tabors were received by the Queen at the Court of St. James where they showed off their new baby daughter, Lillie. On one of those trips they visited the shrine at Lourdes. There, Horace's health improved. His support of his wife's Catholicism was strengthened by this and he began to think about converting. He was still committed to his Masonic brotherhood, but subsequent events as his fortunes dwindled convinced him that his brothers' lack of support, even enjoyment of his downfall, entailed his crossing over to their "enemy" i.e., Catholicism.

The birth of their first child Lillie in 1884 solidified the family circle with its warmth, and Lizzie took on motherhood with her usual zeal. No nannies for wealthy Tabors. (They would later hire tutors to educate their daughter at home.) The gift of emulating her own saintly mother was now her own. In a rare instance of positive newspaper coverage, she managed an interview which testified to her devotion as a mother. Early on, then, there were signs that a driving force for Baby Doe was to restore the Tabor family name, to show that the adverse publicity was a travesty, unjust. Upon her death, tens of thousands of news clippings and other papers saved in sacks and trunks left researchers with the fascinating challenge of reconstructing such truths.

In order to grasp the reality of Lizzie's concern, we must look at one influential source of so-called Tabor "legends." For example, it had been widely publicized that Horace, upon being elected to the U.S. Senate, wore a silk nightshirt on the train to Washington, D.C., elaborately decorated with buttons of brilliant diamonds. A moniker, "Senator Nightshirt," clung to him once this story circulated. After his thirty-day tenure as a Colorado senator expired, Horace was depicted in a news account as roving through the Senate, gathering signatures in an autograph book like some silly high school girl. Upon inspection of his newly built Denver Opera House, Tabor was alleged to have demanded the removal of a portrait of Shakespeare mounted on the wall, and exclaimed, "What did that feller ever do for Denver? Take it down and put up mine in its place." The source of such outrageous caricatures was usually the editor of the *Denver Tribune,* Eugene Field.[20] He wrote a satirical column "All Around Denver," lampooning bigwigs of which Horace Tabor, from 1883-1893, was the biggest of the bigwigs. Accounts of Tabor ordering expensive Paris gowns for his infant daughters and then discarding them after one wearing enhanced the idea that the Tabors were reckless spendthrifts. Lewis Cass Gandy, among the most reliable and objective of Tabor biographers, stated that Eugene Field was "the source of many of the fantastic legends which have grown up around the story of the rise and decline of the Vermont stonecutter, H.A.W. Tabor." The apocryphal story of Shakespeare's portrait grew into an image of Horace as an ignorant philistine. Noting that the "pretentious bit of clothing," the satin nightshirt with diamond buttons, was "Eugene Field's satirical invention," Gandy says, "Field wrote those pieces. . . never thinking they would be remembered. They were." All this was possible because libel lawsuits against newspapers in those days rarely succeeded and because Field scoffed at the idea that anyone would take his jokes seriously. In this, he was tragically mistaken.

In the early 1930s, a writer named David Karsner published a book about Horace, calling him "Silver Dollar." The book that ensued perpetuated the myths created by Eugene Field. Horace was allegedly a hard-drinking, back-slapping, belly-up-to-the-bar sort of guy, ordering drinks for the house—a loudmouth, a gambler, card shark—and the idiot who fiddled while his financial empire burned. This was a legacy of lies spawned by Field's misjudgment, a legacy magnified to the stars when the Hollywood version of Karsner's book, starring Edward G. Robinson, appeared on the silver screen. Repeatedly, Lizzie had been invited to participate and much-needed money offered to her. She declined all these offers and refused to attend the grand social affair at the Denver premier of the movie, but she did send a piece of silver ore to be displayed in the lobby of the theater. How reminiscent of the chunk of ore she once flung at the head of her immature husband, Harvey Doe. How indicative of her pride to refuse Judas money in her poverty.

Journalist Lee Casey lamented this caricature: "[Tabor's] character has not been altered but rather reversed." Casey never met Tabor, but Tabor's friends attested to his character: "He was mild, quiet, even shy." Tabor was caricatured because Field "liked nothing better than to build a straw man and then knock him down."

Field pestered Tabor in two ways. First, he portrayed him as a hell-for leather drinker and gambler—actually Tabor was very abstemious and, until his last years, cared nothing for cards—and then he wrote verses along the line of "roses are red, violets are blue" and printed them in his column under Tabor's by-line. The latter joke so enraged Tabor that, for a few minutes at least, he almost went into a John L. Sullivan rage. . . .Later on, of course, the myth was revived by David Karsner . . . and also of course the misconception was still further exaggerated when Hollywood adapted that work for the screen.

Casey concludes, "It is too bad Denver doesn't have a better understanding of this pious, humble citizen who saved the community [as a builder] from collapse in 1890. . . ." Casey observes that the myth is so widespread that the truth may never catch up. Like Baby Doe, he desires that truths be told so that justice may be done.[21]

Meanwhile, from 1883 until 1893, Tabor's silver mines poured money unabatedly into their coffers with such abundance they never knew precisely what was their net worth. Eight million? Eleven million? No income tax forms were yet required. Most wealthy people were not sure of their income. Nor were they concerned, and they involved themselves in the fatal error of taking it for granted. In later years, Lizzie would tell historian Caroline Bancroft that the need for saving, conserving wealth, did not occur to them. Probably, however, had they conserved some wealth, it would have delayed but not thwarted the day when the estate went into receivership and the court doled out Tabor wealth to individuals who may or may not have deserved it. The 1893 de-monetization of silver and the removal of government price supports constituted a fatal blow to Tabor's fortune. It is worth noting that in 1893 bankruptcy laws were not in place, so that exceptions of some personal belongings, even a house, were not possible then as they might be today. Those who claim that Tabor declared bankruptcy are mistaken. In a receivership, the court held absolute power and the Tabors lost their home and businesses. Personal and household items remained—and significant wealth in Mrs. Tabor's jewelry. The latter she clung to; her daughters would need a dowry in order to marry well. Her Irish Catholic optimism— hope, a virtue—led her to conserve goods for them as she had never thought to do before.

Lizzie watched with indignation and horror the way, by 1896, creditors surrounded the estate like jackals. Her wealthy husband had contributed to the prosperity of the embryonic city of Denver as he built hotels, utilities, a splendid opera house, donated land for the post office, established commercial centers, donated to charitable causes, and much else. He had bank-rolled Colorado's Republican party and mentored many of Denver's foremost citizens into positions of power and money. Now they turned their backs on him, enjoying his downfall, refusing him in his need, denying his largesse. Their perfidy was staggering. She began to save scraps of paper, testimony to a different and truer account she hoped would one day prevail. Her soul shrank as resentment reigned over her spirit.

Just as the scandals, rejection, and shunning of their early days drew this couple closer to one another, this financial disaster solidified their love. Predictions that Baby Doe was merely a gold-digger did not materialize. She remained faithful to her husband and children even when their material wealth disappeared in the terrible years following the de-monetization of silver. The family now included a second daughter, Silver Dollar Rosemary Echo (nicknamed Honeymaid), and they moved into ever more lowly housing until 1898 when Horace was appointed postmaster of Denver. Their fortunes modestly revived, the Tabors moved into a four-room suite at the Windsor Hotel. Signs of Baby Doe's impending reclusiveness emerged, as patrons saw Horace and his two daughters at breakfast in the hotel dining room. A nun from a nearby Catholic school came to pick up the girls, aged 14 and 8, and escorted them to school. Noticeably absent was Baby Doe. What was going on?

The Spring of 1899: Claiming she needed a cure for chronic headaches (neuralgia), Baby Doe took her two daughters and headed for New York where a specialist was supposedly dealing with these symptoms. It seems she left the younger daughter, Silver Dollar, with relatives in Oshkosh and traveled by train with her older daughter Lillie who was suffering from chronic respiratory problems. They took up lodgings in the city. Friends from former affluent years were there, accepting of her in her reduced circumstances. What is known about these months, however, represents a strange story. Baby Doe had brought an artifact with her, a "bone," possibly prehistoric, and tried to sell it, unsuccessfully, to museums. She began to report feelings that she was being stalked and changed her lodgings in response. Was this an indication of the "persecution complex" she had long experienced? Real or imagined? It would be simple to dismiss this as paranoia were it not for another odd development. Horace received a notice from a blackmailer who demanded money in order to keep quiet about his wife's having done a risque dance, the can-can, on a table at some bistro. Horace's aunt Emma Fellows, who was a staunch supporter of Baby Doe and a grim non-supporter of Augusta, the "termagant," had come from her home in Lawrence, Kansas, to housekeep while Lizzie was away. She considered this a complete scam. Horace apparently reacted by losing his temper and claiming, "My wife has never done anything wrong in her life!" No money was sent. Letters, however, were and Horace expected his wife and daughters home by early spring, 1899. Apparently Lizzie replied that some problem with Lillie's eyes meant that they had to remain in New York while the problem was being solved. Horace replied in a letter dated March 23, 1899. "What is wrong with Lillie's eyes?" And he reminds her he has already sent the train fare, making it clear his family is overdue to return home. About the same time, Peter McCourt wrote a sister in Oshkosh that he had urgent business in New York and so would not be in Denver. Was his business to rescue his sister and return her home?

Sometime in late March or early April, Baby Doe and Lillie returned to Oshkosh by train to pick up Silver Dollar. Horace collapsed with his life-ending appendicitis attack in early April and died about a week thereafter, on April 10. Baby Doe was at his bedside as he passed. It is not clear whether she was home by the time her husband collapsed on a Denver street. If she was, it was only a matter of days before. How could this letter of late March have reached her with time still for her to board a train, stop in Oshkosh, and get to Denver? Was it transposed into a telegram? It is merely a letter in a box of correspondence preserved by the Colorado Historical Society. Perhaps it was never sent. Perhaps Baby Doe had some reason to drag her feet about returning to Colorado in the spring. Amid those numberless newspaper clippings is another Baby Doe saved which deals with the problems the ultra-rich have in protecting their families from kidnappers and scam artists. The Guggenheims and Boettchers (who had always treated Lizzie with kindness) knew this just as Baby Doe recalled the vulnerability of her years of prosperity. Stalked and blackmailed, the Tabors could not rid themselves of their former claims to riches, even in 1899.

However, it was Lillie who openly resented the separation those months from her beloved Papa. Perhaps she never completely forgave her mother for their absence from him in the months leading up to his demise. Perhaps this contributed to her alienation from Lizzie and from Colorado, and thus to Lizzie's tragic alienation from her girls.

Once Horace was dead, Denver citizens came in droves to honor their benefactor as they had not done in his need. For Lizzie, this was some satisfaction but perhaps not much as his memory had not been vindicated. There was the Matchless silver mine in Leadville. Although it was mortgaged, the family—reinforced by some expert opinion among Leadville miners and engineers—believed that it might produce significant wealth. Lizzie was left as the executor of Horace's complex estate and as potential owner of the Matchless, a woman in charge of the key to a possible recovery of family fortune. Now began her unfruitful excursions into American capitalism as she sought to salvage assets: the betrayals, greed, the loan manipulation, stock transference, investment in shaky enterprises. She filled a knapsack with ore samples from the Matchless and walked Denver streets seeking investors to share her faith. She found a few and in modest ways, the Matchless mine helped support her and her two daughters.

It is not necessary to go into further detail about the sixteen years of her marriage to Horace Tabor. These were the happiest, most fulfilling years of her life. She was devoted to him and his interests and always referred to him publicly and respectfully as "the Senator."

The Victorian standard for a widow to mourn was two and a half years. After this, Lizzie re-entered society and would later claim she had opportunities to remarry. She elected not to. Probably she had made a more or less formal commitment to a state known as a "consecrated widow." Her acknowledgement to Speaker Longworth that she had "dedicated her life to God" serves as evidence of this.[22] Her decision not to remarry meant that she intended to raise her daughters by herself. Events would show that she was not well-equipped psychologically to do this. Overall, the pattern of her life is tragic, not because she died alone and impoverished at the cabin next to the Matchless mine. Rather, her own paramount value— her family, a loving and unified family—would never be realized.

Victorian Mourning Protocols:

What one should wear and for how long—for widows, the length of time is two-and-one-half years, sub-divided into four periods with various burdens of crape, black silk and half mourning colors. A mother for a child will customarily mourn for one year, six months in deep mourning, thus wearing bombazine & crape for 6 months, black silk for 3 months and half mourning colors for 3 months.

The Victorians of Baby Doe's lifetime used clothing to signify their grief. The great importance of showing respect for their deceased loved ones is evident in the detailed recommendations concerning what to wear and for how long. A widow, for example, would ideally wear her mourning garb for two and one half years, while a mother mourning the loss of a child dressed in black for one year. A widower wore a black suit and mourned his wife in deep mourning for three months. Offspring demonstrated their loss of a parent for one year. The mourning period was divided into sections so that, generally speaking, half the period was marked by deep mourning, one-fourth by "ordinary" mourning in black silk and another one-fourth in half-mourning colors.

Instructions included a careful choice of fabrics: bombazine or crape, black silk, and half mourning colors (e.g., white linen with black trim, cuffs or collars). According to Karen Mchaffey, "Bombazine was a textile with the warp of silk and the weft of worsted that had a twilled appearance. Crape was a transparent crimped silk gauze. These fabrics were suitable for widows in that they lacked shine or luster and provided a solemn appearance for the wearer."

Taken from: The After-Life: Mourning Rituals and the Mid-Victorians by Karen Rae Mchaffey.

Was Lizzie McCourt Doe appearing publically in Leadville veiled and dressed in black because she was ashamed of her illicit liaison with Horace Tabor or because she was mourning the loss of her and Harvey Doe's infant son?

Family was at the core of her being. It remains, therefore, to discuss what family values show about her inner life after the death of her husband. This is best approached by examining her relationships with the three who were closest to her: Lillie, Silver, and her brother Peter. And of these, her daughter Silver provided both the most comfort and the greatest sorrow of her widowhood.

Lillie. Lilllie, nicknamed Cupid, was born July 13, 1884 during the Tabors' prosperous years. Her parents showered her with affection and extravagance. From her earliest years, she could be seen romping in Box A at the Tabor Grand Opera House. Lizzie was proud of her small daughter's ability to play to a camera, posing without coaching. When Lillie was two or three, the acclaimed illustrator Thomas Nast drew a charming picture of Lillie published as the cover for *Harper's Bazaar* magazine. Because of this Lillie became an international child star. Professional photographs of their girl were ordered by the hundreds in order to meet the demand around the world for pictures of Lillie Tabor, the Silver Princess.

In 1902, three years after Horace's death, Lizzie took her girls to visit her family in Wisconsin. Her mother Elizabeth McCourt had suffered a stroke. Lillie wanted to stay to help with her care; Lizzie could not bear separation from her daughters. Lillie, however, was desperate to escape her dreary, confined, impoverished existence next to the Matchless mine or in cheap Denver lodgings. In the face of her mother's obdurate refusal to let her go, she pleaded with Uncle Pete McCourt. He loaned her train fare so she could return to the Midwest—Oshkosh or Chicago. In succeeding years, mother and daughter corresponded about many things and especially about

Lizzie's wishes that her daughter return to Colorado. Although Lillie made vague promises, she never returned. She had found her exile at the Matchless unendurable, her mother and sister unbearable. Bitterly, Lizzie told Leadville historian Edward Blair that Lillie had "turned her back on Leadville." In May, 1908, Lillie eloped with her cousin John Last Jr. Seven months later, Lillie's daughter Caroline was born.

The nineteen year old Silver wrote a reply to the wedding announcement, stating that "Mama is prostrate." The Catholic Church does not allow marriage between first cousins without a special dispensation. In Irish Catholic families, a close watch was kept on cousins living in the same household, but in this case the mother, Lizzie's sister Nealie (Cornelia) McCourt Last, had died of Hodgkins disease and vigilance may have been lax. Lillie, necessarily, married outside the Church. In the years that followed, Lillie admitted "I know how . . . .hateful I have been, but you know that I would die if anything happened to either of you." Lizzie was alternately bitter and conciliatory toward her elder daughter, and Lillie responded in kind. At the end of her mother's life in 1935, Lillie would deny her relationship with that branch of the Tabor family. Thus. the reduced Tabor family boat rocked between the mutual declarations of love and accusations of disloyalty which rained into their hearts via their mailboxes.

Lillie and John Last, Jr. had three children: Carolyn, John Last III, and Jane, born in successive years from 1909 through 1911. Their only son received a degree in engineering, married a woman with a child, and lived out his life in the Hendersonville, North Carolina, area. This family had no other children and the two daughters never married. Thus, Lizzie McCourt Doe Tabor's branch of the family came to an end with the grandson and granddaughters. Horace and Augusta's only son Maxcy carried on the Tabor line.

Thus began Lizzie's process of living for Silver that became a source of tragedy. The protective mother became over-protective; the watchful parent became the source of suffocation. One may dedicate one's life to living for another and awake one day to find the other feels enslaved by your "love."

Honeymaid. Silver Dollar joined the family December 17, 1889, nearly five years after the firstborn Lillie (July 13, 1884). Her reign as a Tabor Silver Princess was brief. She was four when the Tabor estate began to crumble and seven when the family was forced to leave their Sherman street mansion. Although the financial losses would turn out to be irrecoverable, it would be many years before this was a certainty. Rich or poor, however, the family was close. Horace doted on his daughters. Lizzie involved herself with their education, guiding Honeymaid's hands as she learned to form her letters. Baby Doe devoted herself to passing on the traditions of Irish fairy-lore and the spiritual formation of Irish-American Catholicism. With these cultural riches and unconditional love, Silver did not feel the lack of material largesse. However, in April, 1899, when Silver was nine and Lillie fourteen, Papa Tabor died of inoperable appendicitis. The ship of the family listed, and although it did not capsize, it never recovered a completely healthy balance.

Lizzie's fairy child, Silver Dollar, had grown into a high-spirited girl, happy to race about Leadville on her pony named Polly. She had inherited the Irish imagination and the story-teller's gift, but her vision was morbid, reflecting the Gothic spirit of the time. According to Silver's biographer, Leadville writer Evelyn Furman, in 1912 Silver was raped by a Denver attorney. Silver hid this from her mother for three or four years, but her fear of this man "explained" she said, her constant roving around.

Silver sought a literary and journalistic career; there were moments of success. Lizzie watched with pride as Silver bestowed a song whose lyrics she had written upon the visiting celebrity, Teddy Roosevelt (1910). She persuaded friends at the Denver *Times* to hire Silver as a reporter, but she was given only a "sob sister" role, writing for the obituaries and society pages. Occasionally, Silver's verses were published in newspapers, lurid depictions of grey-eyed charmers, devil-may-care trickster figures. Lizzie financed the publication of a

The Tabor cabin near the Matchless mine outside Leadville, Colorado, had been a toolshed. However, it was roomy and heated, providing adequate shelter for Baby Doe.

novella Silver had written called *Star of Blood.* Silver's efforts to sell her book led her to Chicago and a downward spiral of ever more degrading relationships. Her intense desire for a stage career ended with the aforementioned non-speaking part in a movie made in Colorado Springs.

In a memoir entitled "High Altitude Memories," Mattie Edwards Struthman recalled a "short but pleasant friendship" with Silver in the summer of 1902 when both girls were twelve. They met while happening to ride home from Leadville with the local grocery delivery man (Mattie lived ten minutes' walk up the gulch from the Matchless). Finding they had much in common, the girls began taking long walks together, discussing books. Mattie notes:

She [Silver] was obedient to her mother. At first she was not allowed to come into our house, but at the end of that summer she came, after having coaxed her mother into giving her permission. The following summer she was allowed to have picnic lunches with me.
Never once did she apologize for her mother in any way, despite Mrs. Tabor's queer way of dressing and the fact that she lived in the old cabin at the Matchless mine, keeping strictly to herself. [23]

Here is a foreshadowing of the tyrannical protectiveness that would eventually lead the adult Silver to rebel with heart-rending consequences, a life in cheap Chicago hotels, a victim of addictions she could not control.

By 1914, Baby Doe's obedient child had reached 23 years of age and set out on her own, living at the Vendome Hotel in Leadville, formerly the Tabor Grand. In the spring of 1914, she fell in love with a man named Ed, but Baby Doe objected to him. She had agreed to lease the Matchless to him and a business partner but—as usual—changed her mind. It appears her characteristic paranoia about getting cheated came into play. Ed was offended and threatened by Baby Doe's accusations and suspicions and broke off the relationship. Silver was broken-hearted—and went into a towering fury.

"How dare you interfere in my love affairs?" she writes.[24] Telling herself she was saving Silver from a life of sin, Baby Doe spied on Silver's friends and pointed out their shortcomings. Silver wrote in response of "the stench of your constant increasing spying. . . " (Furman 252). In a series of letters written from Leadville lodgings, Silver blamed her mother, also in Leadville, for ruining her life. She described her childhood as devoid of pleasure, impoverished. Her present, she claimed, was a barren waste, her future "a life without happiness or home life or love" (238). "You must realize that you are incapable of supplying in yourself the thrills of gayety and young company which is necessary to a girl my age" (250). Baby Doe had used religion as a weapon as well: "And with it all you solemnly kneel before God in prayer, telling yourself that you are justified in robbing a human being of the most essential things in life and causing overwhelming agony" (253).

Worst of all, beyond the loss of the man she loved, was her sense that her mother was treating her as an object, and she signed a letter "a leaf in the storm." She needed no words to recognize the battle of wills which she was powerless to avoid or to win. Her mother's machinations have "turned me into a machine to please you. . . ." She pled to be treated as a human being, She refered to her mother's "monarchy" and her behavior "in order that your mighty will may be obeyed" (253). That fall Baby Doe surprised Silver during a party at her Denver lodgings, and her friends all fled in panic and embarrassment. Silver informed her mother: ". . . you're going to stop raising hell" (254). And she vowed to have nothing more to do with her. Except for many letters over the next ten years, often signed "Your loving child," Silver kept that vow in spite of herself.

Of course, the folly of an attempt to keep a grown child in close quarters at home meant that Baby Doe couldn't succeed, either. Silver turned to Uncle Pete McCourt and Baby Doe's longtime spiritual advisor, Father Guida (then on the faculty at Regis College), to intervene with her mother. After Silver's flight to Colorado Springs after the raid on her party, Baby Doe asked Uncle Pete to help her get Silver to return home. He replied the next day: "If Silver wants to get married and the man is respectable, I can't see any objection. On the contrary, it is the natural thing to do." He doesn't tell his sister that he's sending Silver money to subsist on. He knew that Baby Doe wanted him to intervene on her terms and only those. Father Guida had also written a supportive letter advising Baby Doe that if Silver and her young man love each other, they should be allowed their relationship. It seems Silver was pregnant and Father Guida recommended the legitimizing of the affair. Baby Doe ignored these voices of reason and it appears she paid for Silver to have an abortion. At least, attempts to find a child put up for adoption during that period of time have proved fruitless and it is assumed that Silver never had the baby.[25]

These extremities of emotion and high drama characterize Baby Doe's life. Wherever she went, she tended to have a divisive effect. Ironically, the charge that she broke up Horace's marriage to Augusta is perhaps the only false example. The battle of wills between her and

Silver in 1914-1915 was typically controversial. "After all, you are her mother," wrote a supportive Denver friend named Ollie. Thus, Baby Doe's interference or intervention in her youngest daughter's life was deemed justified. The problem with this is the implication that no limits on motherhood are appropriate. Has she overstepped a boundary and demanded compliance from an adult child that is no longer a mother's prerogative? At what point does love and respect for grown children as persons mean—if at all—letting go?

However, a second powerful motivation was working in Baby Doe, and that was her determination to restore and maintain the Tabor name to its rightful place historically in Denver as eminent and respectable. She had watched men turn their backs on Horace's needs in 1895-97, men who might have been no-accounts had it not been for her powerful husband's having giving them work and opportunity in the early 1880s. In the face of their blatant and heartless ingratitude, her soul was filled with bitterness. Not even the law of her Catholic faith to forgive enemies could alleviate it. It fell upon her daughters to be pure and righteous in this cause. Her thirst for justice for the family name was a storm in which Silver felt herself a leaf. She was ultimately her own and not her mother's victim, however, and her life subsequently only reminded people of the scandals attached like irremovable barnacles to the Tabor family ship.

At some point, Silver had returned from Colorado Springs and her brief role in a film with the Pikes Peak Film Company, a pre-Hollywood company that flourished briefly until Thomas Edison ran such as them out of business on violations of his patents. In the fall of 1915, Silver worked as a chorus girl in Denver and it was a guarded secret that she had married an underworld figure named Jack la Vode. On September 1, 1915, the *Denver Post* ran an article describing Silver's being held in jail overnight charged with theft. A girl in her company said she had taken her ring. The next day the misunderstanding was all sorted out, and the drunken chorus girls released, but Silver felt great shame and she left Denver never to return. On September 27, 1915, she wrote her mother an explanatory letter from Chicago, describing the debacle. Uncle Phil McCourt of Denver had given her travel money, and she looked for work as a chorus girl in Chicago. Baby Doe's Denver friend wrote her a sympathetic letter agreeing that the whole fiasco was a setup to spite and worry Baby Doe. Ollie says, "...but they might have left the Tabor name out of it." Ollie is responding to Baby Doe's analysis of the drama of the stolen ring as specially designed to spite and worry her. Here again was an instance that her well-known persecution complex manifested itself. The letters of Baby Doe to her daughter are steeped in sentimentality, but her view of Silver's embarrassment in this case is uncharitable, that it was all a ploy to embarrass her mother and besmirch the Tabor family name (Furman 271).

No one knows what happened to Jack la Vode, if he existed, although Silver would use the name Ruth la Vode among her many aliases in the ten years that followed. Most of those years saw her in Chicago, but in 1915 she stayed in Indianapolis, apparently working in vaudeville or burlesque, long enough for her mother to search her out, speak with her doctor about Silver's "illnesses," and demand that her daughter come home to mama. In October of 1915, Silver had had to leave her beloved pony Polly with the livery stable because she could not pay her bill. On October 15, 1915, she wrote that Polly was lost to her. On the 24th of October we learn that that her uncles had refused to send her more money, and it was becoming obvious that Silver used her family's charity to support her addictions. In mid-November, 1915, Baby Doe found Silver, and obtained facts about Silver's "health issues" from her doctor. Silver resented Baby Doe's interference *via* her doctor, and "an embarrassing scene" ensued. Baby Doe went to Wisconsin to confer with Lillie and other family members, who were all upset about Silver's circumstances. Claudia, residing in Chicago, tried to look into her niece's whereabouts, but Silver never visited her though she was close by. There was talk of Lillie's opening her home to Silver, but Silver delayed and Lillie realized at last that her self-destructive sister would not be a good example for her own growing children and by February, 1918, she revoked her invitation. Her father-in-law John Last had come to live with the family, she explained, and the family was crowded.

In her biography of Silver Dollar, Evelyn Furman has transcribed about thirty letters from Silver to her mother from the fall of 1916 until August, 1925, just one month before her death. Silver moved about a great deal as she found work with traveling theatricals. On November 11, 1915, she wrote her mother asking for money, perhaps still in Indianapolis. On January 13, 1916, she wrote from Cleveland, Ohio, where she worked for Dixon's Big Review. By January 28, 1916, she was in Harrisburg, Pennsylvania, and was ill, a surgical patient with a false name by which she hoped her mother could reach her. On February 14, 1916, she was still with Dixon's in Cleveland and described her agonies and physical ailments.

By 1918, she was back in Chicago permanently. In November she wrote to Lizzie telling her that she was homeless, broke, and that she longed to hear news from home. By the beginning of 1919, they were back in contact and a letter in February informed Baby Doe that Silver hadn't heard from Lillie. Silver was still sick. Her ailments over many months had ranged from abcesses which had to be lanced to broken kneecaps and mysterious surgeries. She described steam burns in a letter of January 18, 1925. Her health problems were reasons why she was out of contact. Baby Doe had had a vision of Papa at her home next to the Matchless, and Silver was comforted by this news. Silver's circumstances seem to have improved in 1920 as she sent packages to her mother in August. She wrote in September, saying that two men are crazy about her, but she hasn't much time for men anymore. By January, 1921, she wrote of her ill health again. She was living in the Groveland Park Hotel. All these years she had been using aliases—eight different names in all.

During 1921, Silver seems to have found some stability and retained her Groveland Hotel address most of the year. Her aunt Tillie McCourt Haben and cousin Andrew visited her in February and tried to help with offers to set her up in business. As with other plans to go into business, this fizzled. By April, 1921, she had moved to the Carleton, leaving a bill of $70.00 at the Groveland. Lizzie had written about good dreams she had had, and Silver approved: ". . . maybe they mean that things will change for me." She had moved to the Huntington Hotel by fall and on October 19, 1922, she wrote to her mother, signing herself Ruth Reid. Soon after Baby Doe sent her a small card depicting St. Anthony—the patron of what is lost. Silver thanked her. She wrote again on Christmas, still at the Huntington. Not long after, she had moved to the Grant Park Hotel and wrote, noting to her mother, that "Life is hard." Through all the false names, excuses of illness, cover-ups, she now presented a ray of truth: "Perhaps things might be different if I were different."

In August of 1923, at age 33, she wrote that she had married and was now Mrs. W.J. Ryan. This did not last long, and she informed Lizzie of her divorce from Billy Ryan. In April, 1925, she informed her mother that she and a friend planned to open a dress shop. Now she signed her name R. [Rose] Tabor. Notification of another change of address followed shortly. From yet another address, she wrote in January, 1925, of steam burns she had suffered. The following fall, September, 18, 1925, the newspapers announced her death, a result of severe steam burns and a two-day agony. Silver Dollar Tabor was dead at age 36, in Chicago's tenderloin district, addicted to heroin and alcohol, described as a soiled dove.

Reporters rushed to interview family members, and in Milwaukee a resentful Lillie refused to let them in her home. "I wanted a quiet, decent, sheltered life," she told reporters through a crack in her door. "Why should I, who have pride and position and only like quiet and nice things, have to claim her now in this kind of death?"

This kind of death. Baby Doe had read the newspaper reports, and she knew her sister Claudia had identified the body. She had always despised publicity, and now she must have thought: what right have reporters—nosy parkers—to invade her grief and once again taint the Tabor name with scandal? She told reporters that the woman in Chicago was an impostor. "Silver is in a convent." This sounded outlandish—and perhaps was—to many listeners. However, the depth of her denial under the circumstances is not unheard of. A person who has never suffered the death of an adult child can never quite understand the psychological effects and is in no position to judge whether such denial is part of a larger pattern of mental illness or not. Moreover, her claim was not entirely baseless. A nun, or group of nuns in Chicago, had lent Silver assistance and perhaps temporary shelter. This was publicized by way of a newspaper article in a Denver paper just days after Baby Doe's death in March of 1935. The headline reads: "'Baby Doe' Tabor leaves Religious Articles to Nun." The text reads:

'Sister Florence' of a Chicago convent, has three prayer books, some rosary beads and a small cross awaiting her here, left by Mrs. Tabor. Orville Proulx, 17, senior at St. Francis De Sales school said the articles were given him by Mrs. Tabor. . . to give to Sister Florence because she once befriended Mrs. Tabor's daughter Silver Dollar when she was ill in Chicago years ago. "I had often corresponded with Mrs. Tabor," Orville said. "She sent the religious articles to me by another woman for 'Sister Florence'. I have never been able to locate her but I have the articles and will send them if I can." [26]

No more specifics have come to light, and perhaps Sister Florence never received Baby Doe's marks of gratitude. However, somehow (perhaps through her sister Claudia) she learned of this connection and likely had it in mind when she insisted to reporters and writers that Silver was in a convent.

Peter McCourt, Jr.: Uncle Pete. Of all those whom Horace befriended among his wife's family, Peter McCourt made the most of his opportunities. He was affable, charming, outgoing, and popular. He enjoyed a long career as a theater manager in Denver, first at the Tabor Grand and later at his own place, the Broadway Theater. He married successfully, being a good husband and stepfather. However, this brother, who had been Lizzie's favorite playmate all through childhood, disappointed his older sister in many ways, betraying Lizzie's idea of family loyalty. For example, when Lizzie was first married, she suffered social ostracism, as we have seen. Peter displeased her by inviting the husbands of women who shunned her into the Tabor mansion for card games. Her objections fell on deaf ears. Brother and sister had worked together well at the theater during the prosperous years, but when the Tabor empire began to collapse, Peter refused to put his own money down as a bailout. Wisely, he saw that he could not save Horace's business enterprises, but Lizzie, of course, saw this as a sign of ingratitude since Horace had set Peter on his road to success in the first place.

The rupture in their relationship which could not be healed, though, resulted from Uncle Pete's role in helping Lizzie's adult daughters, giving them money and advice and in general responding to their expressed need for a substitute father. Since Lizzie resented his "interference," although even she herself sought his help, Peter was in a difficult position. He often attempted to stay out of the picture, only to accede to what seemed Lillie's or Silver's desperation. Leadville residents observed that Lizzie never forgave Peter for helping Lillie or Silver in their quests for independence from her. Her proud refusal to have anything further to do with him led him to subterfuge.

Lizzie had written Peter off as a personal enemy and—stubborn, stiff-necked and proud—vowed never to take a penny from him. But, during the years the Matchless was leased to W.

Casey, the books would reflect expenses owed by Mrs. Tabor. Mr Casey, Griswold reports, would reveal these amount to Uncle Pete, (a successful theater manager) who would then give him twenty dollars or thereabouts for Lizzie. "Casey. . . always gave Mrs. Tabor the amount of money she needed, usually fifteen or twenty dollars at a time, recording the amount in a special ledger which he kept; then, whenever he went to Denver on business, he would meet with Mrs. Tabor's brother, Peter McCourt. . . and McCourt would pay him whatever amount was in the ledger since the last time they had met." The article goes on to mention that these transactions, carried out between 1913-1917, were somewhat clandestine "so McCourt could help his sister financially since she would not accept any money from him directly after he had been an ally to Lillie when she had left her mother." [27]

The final insult to Lizzie arrived in the form of a legacy. Peter McCourt, Jr. left her a block of carriage stock and when he predeceased her in 1929, she found herself the proud part-owner of a company prosperous in the horse and buggy days. She responded with cynicism, having come to expect nothing but bad news about brother Peter. So he left her a worthless legacy? What else was new?

Other of her McCourt siblings never went public about the problems their Beauty Queen sister caused to the family. We have seen that their father suffered spiritually from the role he had played in that Washington wedding of 1883. She had apparently been somewhat spoiled by her parents as they spared her household chores. "Peaches" would not suffer the fate of an Irish washerwoman. When her older sisters were married, their lovely younger sister would steal the show. The family probably never forgot the occasion of their eldest daughter Margaret's wedding to Wm Courtney when, at the reception, the groom swept the teenaged Baby into his arms and kissed her passionately. The bride, Maggie, embarrassed and humiliated by this, created a scene. The incident caused Lizzie so much shame that even in her 70s she dreamt about it, as we know because she marked it on her calendar: "dreamt Courtney kissed me." These dreams involved his spying through her windows like a peeping tom. Thus, Maggie's horror—other sisters' outrage—meshed with Lizzie's feelings of being stalked and her nightmares decades later memorialized these experiences. We are reminded again of her divisive effect, an outcome of her "Irish wilfulness," on situations where she would have preferred to bring family closer. We are also reminded that she did not welcome the stares of all the strange men whose attentions, though understandable, she experienced as intrusive.

Lizzie maintained a solid relationship with her brother Phil McCourt, in part because he was not part of her scene as her daughters' mother. Her younger sister Claudia was a staunch supporter. Her younger brothers Stephen and Mark McCourt provided modest financial support from time to time. Thus, her relationship with the McCourt brothers, excepting Pete, was generally cordial and especially close with Claudia McCourt McCabe.

During the decades between Horace's death in 1899 and Silver's death in 1925, Baby Doe sifted through business papers, hoping for recoverable assets from the tangled estate of which she was executrix. She became adept at writing contracts and assessing accounts. Only the Matchless mine, star of the Baby Doe legend, provided some income. It was not enough to sustain the operation long-term, but it was, as it turned out, all she had. Her fight to "hang onto the Matchless" provided journalists, novelists, even opera librettists, with the material for sensational drama. According to such accounts, Baby Doe waged a heroic struggle, doomed to failure but carrying out the deathbed command of her husband to "hang on to the Matchless; it will produce millions again."

A lively debate has gone on in the past two decades since Carolyn Bancroft admitted that the famous phrase was her invention and that everyone knew her history was somewhat fictionalized. Horace's son Maxcy Tabor claimed that no such phrase had been uttered in his hearing. However, in an interview with Lizzie's brother, Phil McCourt, just days after her death, Phil told reporters: "Tabor used to say, 'We must hold on to the Matchless, Phil. There is still money in it.' And that is what he said when he died. Did you know that? When he died he told Elizabeth to hold on to it." Bancroft was apparently unaware that the source of that part of the Tabor legend had this testimonial supporting it, and she needlessly conceded a point of history with damage to her own reputation.[28]

Lizzie's faithfulness to a deathbed mandate, so central to her legend, is not so much false as perverted—attributing to her secular and materialistic motives, interpreting her hopes for a livelihood from the mine outside the context of her core values on family and a devout life. Readers who wish to understand her relationship with the Matchless mine should examine it through the lenses of her character and values as discussed in the next section. In addition, her legend should be regarded skeptically insofar as it imputes false motives to her.

Griswold's *History of Lake County* reports on the legal history of the Matchless as follows:

According to the Ballenger and Richards directories: W.F. Page, who had managed the Matchless for several years prior to and after Tabor's death, also was manager of the property from 1904 to 1909; T.M. Ramey was listed as the manager for 1910; and G.W. Casey, who was an insurance agent, was listed as lessee of the mine from 1913 to 1917. No managers or lessees were listed for the years of 1909, 1911, 1912 or 1918.[29]

Whatever promise the Matchless mine held would be cancelled by the Depression and finally thwarted by Mother Nature as flooding became a serious problem.

At first, however, Baby Doe shared Horace's opinion that the Matchless held promise. It was common knowledge. Local miners and other experts encouraged Baby Doe that the Matchless had potential for zinc, sulfides, or silver.

Although the Matchless did yield moderate returns, water often seeped into the tunnels, causing the operation to suspend while they were pumped. When expenses outran income, another mortgage would have to supply capital. On one occasion her sister Claudia McCourt McCabe paid off debt in return for collateral, Baby Doe's jewelry. When no more mortgages were available, and the miners couldn't be paid, Baby Doe would attempt to run the machinery herself, donning work clothes and scampering up and down the ladder of the central mine shaft.

The financial history of Baby Doe and the Matchless came to a resolution in 1928 when the John K. Mullen family of Denver paid the liens and taxes on the property. Their Hungarian flour company having enriched them, they were a prominent Catholic philanthropic family. They granted Baby Doe her cabin next to the mine as a permanent home. Although she had resented the Mullen interest initially, upon hearing of the foreclosure, Baby Doe told reporters that she had another five years during which she could pay back her $14,000 loan on the Matchless. Countering claims that she resented Mullen's actions, she told the reporters: "I told him [J.K. Mullen] to foreclose in order to clear the title of the mine." And Griswold sums up: "Rather than have his name connected with the foreclosure against the Tabors, whose very great friend he had been all his life, he organized the Shorego Mining Company, of which he is the principal stockholder." After John Mullen's death, his estate representatives reassured Mrs. Tabor that she was entitled to live at the Matchless as long as she desired.[30] Anyone who hoped to see Baby Doe let go of her mine kicking and screaming, as the legend suggests, saw, instead, a resignation, even, perhaps, a reconciliation to reality.

This sounds like a graceful letting go and an acceptance, not of a failure, but of something that no longer gave meaning to her life. The Matchless represented material hopes, but in the last decade of her life, she turned to spiritual themes, looking inward, no longer questing for worldly success. If family was a pillar of her inner life, her relationship to God was the other one.

Atropos:
Circumstances of Death

*I*n the preceding chapters, we have seen how Lizzie's childhood environment and experiences paved the way for her future. By establishing core values of family and faith, her Oshkosh parents provided her the yardsticks to measure her life's successes and failures. We have seen why the public judged her a sinner and how her hopes for flourishing family relationships failed. By 1925 her way of life focused on devotions and detachment. Gradually, she snipped the threads of her attachments to things and persons, facing her own mortality, creating the circumstances of her death. Death, as an event, is the culmination of this process. Now, on that wintry day in 1933, as she trudged into Leadville, she carried within her a mixture of emotions which had come under the governance and discipline of her Catholic faith in a complex relationship of Irish Catholic practice with its "folk religion" language of signs and the Jesuit influence upon her spirituality, fulfilling her middle name, Bonduel.

As young Helen Skala pondered her father's words: "There is one of the most famous people in all of Colorado history," Helen was inclined, with a child's open curiosity, to wonder how the poor, decaying old woman could have inspired such awe. Others who would have seen Mrs. Tabor might not have been so charitable. To many in Denver and some in Leadville who believed that Baby Doe had wrecked Horace's marriage in order to marry for money, this pathetic figure represented one who deserved such a downfall.

Many writers have commented on her queer way of dressing, wearing on her feet gunny sacks instead of galoshes against the deep snows, attributing this to her poverty, as though she possessed no better.[31] At least one writer, however, connects this correctly to her status as a penitent. "She was a bizarre figure when she appeared on the streets [of Leadville] in her old duster, wearing men's shoes and carrying a carpet bag. Those years, the biggest share of her life, were years of bitter penance."[32] On her head she wore a motoring (or bicycle) cap. Although this was not strictly a masculine style, her choice of headgear, like her choice of winter footwear, would be listed as part of her eccentricity. For a penitent it had the advantage of a bill which could support a veil if desired. An article in a 1953 edition of the *Denver Catholic Register* reiterates this: "Baby Doe Tabor, despite the fact that she committed many sins as a younger woman, spent the last part of her life as a true and devoted Catholic. She retired to a life of penance and self-mortification at the Matchless Mine cabin in Leadville."[33] She herself testified to something of this sort in a letter to U.S. Representative Nicholas Longworth. She wanted Representative Longworth to help her recover the old Denver Post Office site which Horace had donated to Denver, and she assures him of her integrity and good faith, stating, "I am espoused to God and always will be."[34] Occasionally, she gave hints as to her changed ways; when curious citizens might dare inquire what her former life had been like, she would reply: "I am a better person now." Other than that, she refused to converse about that other life she had led as the Silver Queen of the West.

Once a curious child in Leadville had asked Mrs. Tabor, "Why do you always cover your pretty hair?" (That legendary, lush strawberry blonde.) The young Teresa O'Brien says she "felt a bony hand on my shoulder. Those violet eyes gazed at me intently. 'My dear, when one is penitent one must sacrifice, and that's the way I do it, keeping my beauty covered.' "[35]

As a sign of similar sacrifice, she had detached herself from worldly possessions, no longer caring for the beautiful clothes that had once delighted her. Even her jewelry, her last resort from poverty, had gone to cover her debt to her sister Claudia McCourt McCabe or was left carelessly with other items in her trunks at St. Vincent's. The power she had had to turn heads wherever she went now meant nothing. Although her "legend" often leads us to believe that she clung to the Matchless to some bitter end, the fact is that even her struggle to hang on to the Matchless mine had ceased when the Mullen family cleared the title.[36]

Everyone who knew her well had heard her say she no longer cared for the things of this world and could see that she lived out this principle. Such a process of conversion from rampant worldliness to penitent recluse involves a profound worldly detachment. To summarize her detachment, she kept a poem, "The World's a Hollow Bubble," a verse found in 1935 among one of the trunks she stored with the Sisters of Charity, at St. Vincent's hospital in Leadville.[37] "Just a piece of painted trouble. . . we come on earth to cry. . . just a nightmare in the dark." All life is empty routine, including business, love, politics, "Clubs and parties, cliques and sets, /Fashions, follies, cigarettes." All this wisdom Baby Doe had passed along to Silver, who included it in her 1911-12 publication *Star of Blood*; "No peace but in the grave," her heroine, a reformed party girl suspiciously like Baby Doe, reflects.

Among Lizzie's friends were the Sisters of Charity of Leavenworth who had a small convent in Leadville. They had established St. Vincent's hospital there and helped the poor and sick. They provided Baby Doe with a broom handle painted black to look like the business end of a shotgun. Baby Doe could point that through a small opening in her cabin door in order to intimidate unwelcome callers. Later on, when her neighbor, one Mr. George Schmitt, passed on, she inherited his gun and could brandish the real thing. Apparently, she never fired it.

The Sisters offered her free storage of her trunks, which, after her death, proved to hold items of value, showing that her poverty was a product of her conscious choice. The Sisters also provided food, moral support, friendship, prayers and other small favors. It must have been a relief to Lizzie to have these women watching her back in her later years, women less likely to raise up her persecution complex, women like herself who were espoused to God.

The silence surrounding her penitential status was broken after her death, as many then felt free to speak out. Among these was the man who, himself Irish Catholic, shared her world view, the local priest. A few blocks away from E. 5th Street stood the Church of the Annunciation and the rectory from which Fr. Edward Horgan shepherded his flock. Whenever he noticed a light on or heard a rustling late at night at the church next door, he knew it was Baby Doe who came to pray and light votive candles at odd hours. Father Horgan told a *Rocky Mountain News* reporter that he had known Baby Doe "quite well," and "we'd talk about religion."[38]

He does not give specifics, but we know many of the issues which interested her, and these primarily involved close family members. Given the sordid circumstances of Silver's death, was there hope of heaven for her? If Silver had repented of her sins during her final days, she would have been taken into heaven. She also considered Horace's deathbed reception of the sacraments from Father Gubiposi. Did this not indicate immediate acceptance into heaven, so that her beloved husband was a saint? The precedent for this Catholic doctrine was based on the words of Jesus from the cross to the good thief Dismas on the occasion of his last-moment conversion: "This day thou shalt be with Me in Paradise." In his book *The Saga of H.A.W. Tabor,* Rene L. Coquoz, a Leadville citizen, explains the circumstances. Coquoz writes that "Tabor Converted to Catholicism."

It was about two weeks before Tabor's death that he decided to join the Catholic faith. Friends of Mr. Tabor were not surprised, as his wife was a devout Catholic. He was to have gone to the Sacred Heart Church at 28th and Larimer Streets on the Tuesday before he became ill [April 6, 1899]. When he became ill, he asked his wife to summon the Reverend Father Gubiposi of the Jesuit Order of Priests to come and baptize him in preparation for entering the Catholic faith. Mrs. Tabor, however, told her husband that it would be much better to wait until he was well and able to go to the church. Her husband agreed with her, but when he became worse it was decided not to wait, and Mrs. Tabor summoned Father Gubiposi.

Mr. and Mrs. Tabor had made a European trip before Tabor began to lose his fortune. They visited many parts of Europe, including the famed Lourdes Grotto in France. After the visit to the Grotto, Tabor was helped greatly in his hearing. His sense of hearing had been growing worse and more defective as time went on. The visit to the Grotto helped him to the extent that he was no longer hard of hearing and Tabor felt so grateful that when he returned to the United States, he expressed his desire to become a Catholic.

The Tabor's donated considerable sums of money to various Catholic institutions and elsewhere in their more prosperous years. Many distinguished clergymen visited with the Tabor's in their mansion in Denver.[39]

Speaking of Horace's conversion during a eulogy at his funeral, Father Barry claimed that "He was not a death-bed convert, although the form was then [at his deathbed] applied. But the principles had been installed in him many years before. Many a time had the priests discovered him alone before the altar paining out his soul in silent prayer to his God above."[40]

Baby Doe was also interested in the Spiritualist movement in America and was herself a medium for visionary experiences which

Lizzie Tabor claimed her Bible was her favorite "readable." This copy belongs in her cabin which is now a historic site overseen by the National Mining Museum, Leadville, Colorado.

will be discussed subsequently. Thus, quite likely, she also discussed with Father Horgan her experiences as a visionary.

For his part, Father Horgan reminded Baby Doe that, as Horace's widow, she was free to return to the sacraments and full participation in the Catholic church. Yet he says he never saw her at the sacraments. She was not one to congratulate herself on her piety, and she realized that a public show of marching to the communion rail would remind the faithful of her hypocrisy. For her, to be Catholic meant to cultivate an intense prayer life and pursue privately certain spiritual exercises.

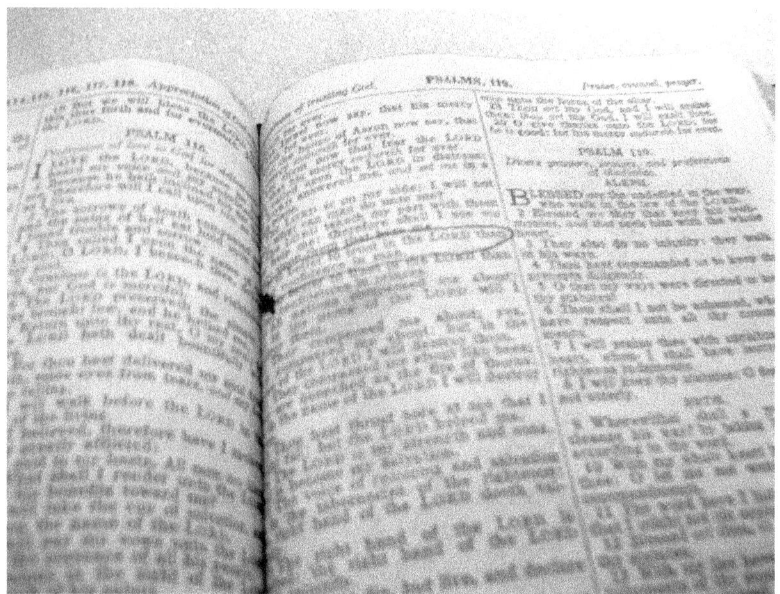

Lizzie's underlinings in her Bible often referred to themes about the protection God gives—and how God takes care of one's enemies.

Church visits were but one of many devotional practices. The Bible was one of two favorite "readables," (the other being her cookbook) and she sometimes annotated hers in the margin. Her Bible, now preserved at the historic cabin next to the Matchless mine, contains several passages she underlined. From these, we see what she meant when she declared herself to be "espoused to God." Psalm 118:8: "It is better to trust in the Lord than put confidence in man." And, "for the Lord your God he it is that fighteth for you as he has promised you. Take heed, therefore, unto yourselves that ye love the Lord your God." (Joshua 24: 10-11) The following quotation also emphasizes her concept of God as defender, protector and refuge: "The eternal God is thy refuge. . . and he shall thrust out the enemy from before thee, and shall say, destroy them. (Dt 34: 27)

She had created a rosary out of shoestring, knotted fittingly for the prayers. Father Horgan offered her a proper rosary, but this rustic set of "beads" suited her. If people approached her while she prayed, she could quickly hide her shoelace and avoid, she hoped, appearances of hypocrisy. Her homemade rosary, with a black cross dangling from it, often adorned her neck and was an emblem of her late life spirituality, the devotion, privacy, self-imposed poverty.

Among the books left in her cabin after her death was one titled *The Old Gray Rosary.* The author writes of the proper rosaries she owns:

> I keep them put away as sacred souvenirs of religion and friendship, but have never used them for devotional purposes, because they are too showy. . . .It might distract others, though, to see the glitter and hear the jingle of such beads; then when attention is attracted to them might not you feel just a little vain-glorious at having them?[41]

Apparently Baby Doe took a lesson from this book. Gunny sack overshoes and shoestring rosaries announced her rejection of vain-glory.

Thus, by 1933, as she passed the window of the Skala family on her way to town that winter day, her errands were simple and inexpensive. She would stop at the post office, for she might have a letter to send or mail to collect, as there was always the slim chance of a letter from her Milwaukee daughter, Lillie, or even a miracle—word from or about Silver Dollar whose death eight years earlier she could not completely accept. She often got letters from fans and friends. She might order coal to supplement what she gathered along the railroad tracks, or purchase a few groceries, just enough, friends recalled, "to keep body and soul together." Her youthful, melodious voice, (like the chime of a bell) would be heard and recognized. Her beauty had faded but was not altogether gone, as fellow shoppers could see. She might next stop at the library to read the latest newspapers. Zaitz' grocery boy, Elmer Kutzlub, often bundled Mrs. Tabor into the delivery wagon, drove her through the snow, and deposited her at the cabin doorstep. If the snow was mid-winter deep, he would carry her from wagon to doorstep.[42]

The cabin, too, was testimony to her abject poverty, but it was not without its homeyness. Elmer Kutzlub, sometimes invited in for cookies and hot chocolate, reported that the cabin was always clean and neat. The cabin was warm and many, many people in those Depression years had much less. She knew that she could have lived in a suite at Leadville's Vendome Hotel built by Horace Tabor, formerly the Tabor Grand, as quarters had been reserved. Helen Skala reports: "When the Tabor Grand Hotel was built on the corner of Harrison Avenue and Seventh Street in Leadville, it contained a Tabor Suite. At any time during her lifetime, Baby Doe could have moved into these rooms."[43]

She refused goods and offers that smacked of charity. Her stiff-necked refusal to accept charity seemed to challenge her fans to offer various kinds of well-intentioned assistance. Her cabin next to the Matchless became a sort of shrine where visitors left offerings. Docents at the Matchless mine in Leadville tell of local lore: Visitors sometimes left offerings of food, clothing, etc. at her gate, twenty yards or so from her cabin. Baby Doe would sort through, save what she fancied, and return the remainder as unwelcome charity.

The renowned Colorado writer, Frank Waters, left her a bag of oranges on his way back from California. In his book about the Colorado River, Waters recalls trudging up Fryer hill, accompanied by his sister Naomi. Waters notes that during the 1880s and early '90s, silver mining "had made. . . [the Matchless mine] one of the most fabulous spots on the American continent and this woman [Lizzie Tabor] an international toast." Like many before him, Waters perceived a gun's black muzzle pointed out a crack in the door. In a "sepulchral voice out of a sepulchral past," Baby Doe, then nearly 80, having lowered the gun, commented that Naomi was "kind of pretty. It goes with a good heart." She hoped that Naomi was not a newspaperwoman, and—speaking of journalists—remarked "that's all that come up here anymore." Baby Doe complained of them as "Lyin', thieving scoundrels. . . .None of them with the good, simple heart of Mr. Tabor."[44]

An amusing recollection published in the *Rocky Mountain News* in 1968 tells of the Joseph Iacino family's visits to Leadville. Joe had been recently married and had long heard stories about the legendary Baby Doe from his mother, a friend of one of the Tabor servants. The first time he was granted a visit to Mrs. Tabor, he took gifts, including fried chicken, a chocolate cake his mother had baked, a bottle of whiskey. His new wife was not with him on that occasion, but subsequently Mrs. Tabor granted the couple permission to visit once again. This time Joe's new bride witnessed Lizzie opening a trunk and "Mrs. Iacino saw a trunkful of candy and stale cakes that had been sent to her. 'I wondered if Joe's mother's cake was there,' she said."[45] Baby Doe was detached from indulgence in cakes but not, it would seem, from "ale" or, better, whiskey. From time to time,

Iacino, who was in the business, would leave a complementary bottle for Baby Doe—one she accepted as "medicine."

After her death, stacks of such donations—clothes, shoes, galoshes, food, etc.—were discovered in and behind the cabin. Friends were aware that, when possible, she returned items, so these represented anonymous gifts. Had she cared about the image she projected on the Leadville streets, she could have accepted these thoughtful donations. Perhaps not only pride, but worldly detachment, motivated her to put them aside. However, the picture of the lonely, old widow living without charitable gifts must be modified somewhat. For, in spite of her careless attitude toward her benefactors, she lived on charity offered by family members, local Leadville businesses and others who stooped to give it without her knowledge, such as that offered by her brother, Peter McCourt, discussed above. This view is also somewhat modified by her willingness to accept assistance from the John K. Mullen family. On the occasion of her death, shocked citizens criticized the McCourt family and Leadville citizens for allowing the old lady to die in such squalid circumstances. Brother Willard McCourt, however, pointed out that despite repeated family attempts to help her, she accepted charity only from the Mullen family.

Her remaining next to the Matchless was significant because it was her spiritual place. If the spirit of Horace were ever to grace her consciousness or a letter by or about her beloved daughter Silver to arrive, it would not reach her in a Denver boarding house, but here—her traditional home, next to the flooded Matchless mine. Here she could dream of loved ones, record those dreams, and hope for a traditional Irish "dream-out," the stamp of reality on a dream.

No change of address would, in these circumstances, benefit her. In her very late 70s, she received a letter from a woman she did not know—who called herself Sue Bonnie but whose real name was Naomi Poitiers. Sue Bonnie wanted to come, share the cabin, care for the legendary Baby Doe. Wisely, Baby Doe, although she was "losing it," did not accept the offer. The disreputable young woman with the many tattoos (viewed with grave suspicion by Leadville citizens) moved to a nearby cabin and became part of Baby Doe's "spiritualist" activities with a ouija board. The temptation to communicate with Silver was important. Baby Doe was also a type of "medium" *vis a vis* the spirit world. Her experience with spirits is discussed below.

Like so many women whose heart has been pierced by many swords, Baby Doe had a special devotion to the Blessed Virgin Mary. In summer, she decorated a little shrine on her dresser with wildflowers and in winter with evergreen boughs. As so often happened, her religious practices led to misunderstandings. Since many days passed between her death and the discovery of her body, the evergreens to the Virgin had turned brown, a sign, latecomers thought, of her mental illness. Who would put up dead evergreens in the cabin? Many, however, knew better. When a committee of Leadville citizens, chaired by Denver historian Carolyn Bancroft, determined to restore Baby Doe's cabin in 1953, they sought replicas of her holy pictures, including Hoffman's portrait of Jesus at the age of twelve, one of the Holy Family, one of the Ascension, and a picture of the Virgin Mary, crowned Queen of Heaven, framed in Mexican tin.[46]

Her relationship with the Virgin Mother must have been deeply intimate. Baby Doe reported having experienced consolations from the Virgin as a series of spiritual favors. Whether these were "visions" or felt interiorly without sense perception, we do not know. In at least one instance, she did "see" the Virgin and made a rough drawing. She bore witness to such favors so that her inner circle of friends came to respect her deep piety. They did not pass judgment on the authenticity of her visions. It would not have been appropriate. Their own piety acknowledged the same realities that she knew, with or without visionary experience.

Nonetheless, her claims regarding spiritual favors and visions have troubled biographers who were sometimes inclined to interpret these as more evidence of her derangement. While contemporary people may tend to be skeptical, it is anachronistic to impute this to the world of Baby Doe. People often have religious experiences. Sometimes visions are given unexpectedly but are accepted by religious people as genuine and meaningful. In spite of secularism, materialism, skepticism, ordinary people usually were open to these in many forms in the first half of the twentieth century in America. Irish women considered "fey" a gift with which all were familiar if not blessed.

Catholics in general, and Irish Catholics especially, take the communion of saints seriously. Holy people are powerful mediators when one needs supernatural solutions to everyday problems. Baby Doe had found an affinity with St. Teresa of Avila, whom she described as her favorite. Teresa's life story revealed a youth of spiritual carelessness. She was a nun, but her community set bad examples, socializing through the day without thought of Christ and his Church. In these frivolous times, Teresa thought whatever she did could be no worse than what everyone else in her community did, and so she rationalized what she later deemed "wickedness." In Butler's *Lives of the Saints,* he says, "She had not yet the courage to renounce dissipation of time and gifts." But she found this courage, and a process of withdrawal from the social whirl led her to desire to become a hermit. She experienced a "disrelish of the things of this world." She deeply regretted the frivolity of those early years. This was a process of genuine conversion, a turning around from one's former self, walking a path to spiritual perfection toward God. Despite Teresa's unworthiness, she experienced spiritual favors, *gratis*, from God, and in addition to levitation, she was granted visions. The source of such visions was at issue, of course, because the Devil can simulate holy visions. Much of Teresa's autobiography concerns attempts to sort out whether her visions were of divine origin. Her spiritual advisors were not always of one opinion on the subject, and she endured persecution from those who doubted her visions. Butler explains: "After [Teresa] had finally withdrawn . . . from the pleasures of social intercourse and other. . . faults, [she] was very frequently favored by God. . . with intellectual visions and interior communications. The warning of women who had been miserably duped by. . . the Devil much impressed her, and. . . she was perplexed. . . ."[47]

Another powerful sign for Baby Doe was Teresa's role as a mother, the abbess of a convent responsible for her "daughters." As Teresa was called to found a new order, she yearned for her lost daughters in the old convent (those who elected not to join her) even though some of these had rebelled against her authority. In the new convent, strict rules of poverty and enclosure reigned. Only through the generosity of a wealthy widow did this reformed Carmelite convent survive.

All this would have been available to Baby Doe through Butler's three and one half page description of Teresa's life in *The Lives of the Saints,* which Baby Doe studied. Perhaps she read the entire *Autobiography*. Whatever the source, Baby Doe saw her own life pass before her eyes as she learned about Teresa of Avila: the party girl who eventually longed to be a hermit; the spendthrift who had come to value poverty; the disappointed mother whose daughters (in a convent where she was abbess) rebelled against her; her rejection and persecution because of spiritual favors; her "disrelish for" the things of this world; her encounters with spirits whose source posed a problem: heaven or hell? She identified with the wealthy widow who financed Teresa's foundation of a severely cloistered and impoverished convent. If the Matchless yielded its promise, a once-again wealthy Tabor woman could finance such an enterprise. As noted in an article from the *Denver Catholic Register* of April, 1935, describing a not-so-recent visit from Baby Doe to their offices: "She declared that religion had become the greatest solace of her life, and she hoped for a return of part of her fortune only that might be able to make great gifts to the works of the Catholic Church."[48]

Among the odd assortment of newspaper clippings she saved was an article entitled "Sacraments Given 80 Feet in Air."[49] One is inclined to consider her valuing this enough to save it as a sign of how "odd" she was. However, on second thought, it is possible that this report motivated her to ask Father Horgan, as they talked about religion, what he thought of such phenomena. In any case, her avowed devotion to St. Theresa of Avila, made the idea of levitation real to her. Butler's *Lives of the Saints* explains, "In raptures she was sometimes lifted in the air." The busy Abbess at the Convent of

St. Joseph in Avila found her work interrupted by such "spiritual favors"—not always welcome to St. Teresa, however remarkable. Here is another example of the benefits of looking at Baby Doe's life through the lens of her Catholicism and her particular devotions and spiritual interests. By itself, her saving that clipping makes no sense, but in the context of her religion, and her devotion to St. Teresa, it can make sense.

Baby Doe was known in Leadville as a visionary. Teresa O'Brien, whose mother knew Baby Doe well, described her as a "mystic."[50] Seeing this in a more negative light, the Tabor biographer Lewis Gandy says the late-life Baby Doe "succumbed to mysticism." Regarding her visionary experience as a weakness (a symptom of derangement), creates a prejudice, however, that does not help us understand how they functioned in her life. Through her religious experiences, we find two important aspects of Baby Doe's identity. She was a devout Catholic and a visionary. One can certainly be one without the other. The term "vision" is broad. It may refer to one's nighttime dreams, daydreams, hypnogogic states, epiphanies, peak experiences, encounters with ghosts, locutions, and mystical raptures as described in the biographies of saints such as Teresa of Avila. However, it is important to realize that her interest in her dreams (of which there is a great deal of evidence) should be regarded as a different kind of experience from her visions of other-worldly figures. Accordingly, I will treat them separately.

Lizzie's life as a visionary—or medium—was no secret among the citizens of Leadville, and apparently she spoke freely about these experiences. Her visions included religious figures such as Jesus and Mary as well as "devils" and "angels," who seem to be other-worldly figures. On at least one occasion she "saw" Horace near the Matchless mine, as we know since daughter Lillie replied in a letter, noting that she was happy to hear it. Significantly, there is no record of an encounter with Silver. Perhaps this absence contributed to Lizzie's hope that Silver was not deceased. Teresa O'Brien's mother occasionally gave Baby Doe rooms 1 and 2 in her boarding house. She once complained that Baby Doe spent all night "talking to someone in the spirit world." She resented this because it kept the other lodgers awake all night.[51]

Teresa gives no indication others considered that Baby Doe, the "mystic," suffered from mental illness, but many people have associated her visionary life with madness. Thus, her biographers refer to her as "the madwoman," or to a process of her "going mad next to the Matchless." It has been suggested that her water supply was tainted with poisonous and mind-destroying elements such as lead or mercury. (The Mad Hatter of *Alice in Wonderland* is a stock character whose occupation—making hats—involved the use of mercury and resulted in the overthrow of the hatter's sanity.)

In the preceding pages, I have introduced a fair amount of testimony from those who saw her as mentally alert, balanced, and able to manage her own affairs. The plea of her brother Phil McCourt echoes: "Don't let them say. . . she had wild ideas." Where is the truth which will serve her biography best? We may never know. However, the viewpoint represented by her parish priest, Father Horgan, upon the topic of religious visions, may show us how Baby Doe herself regarded them. Since he and Baby Doe talked about religion on numerous occasions, what would have been his response to her visionary experiences? He no doubt understood the attitude of the Roman Catholic Church toward the subject.

The Church, contrary to what some may think, does not readily validate reported sightings in the appearances of religious figures. If the visions achieve widespread popular support, an investigation may be warranted. The Church sends a "Devil's Advocate"; his job is to bring a healthy skepticism to the report. Unless there is compelling evidence to the contrary—such as the healing waters at Lourdes in France—judgment is suspended. On the other hand, innumerable encounters with other-worldly figures mark the experience of people throughout the ages, from the ends of the earth. The Church, as Father Horgan could have explained, expresses no opinion on their authenticity even as she recognizes the possibility for their occurrence.

The current situation in Medjugore, BosniaHerzgovina, where reported sightings of the Virgin Mary have aroused widespread interest, offers a timely example. A religious order now offers a pilgrimage around the area. Their Website—www.ourladycalls.com—contains the following caveat:

In conformity to the decree of Pope Urban VIII, and the directives of the Vatican Council II, Our Lady Calls Pilgrimages to Medjugore [copyright] declares that we do not have the intention to precede the judgement of the Roman Catholic Church in regards to the validity of the supernatural character of facts and messages related to the reported events in Medjugore. This judgement belongs to the authority of the Church, to whom we submit ourselves fully. Words used in any of Our Lady Calls Pilgrimages to Medjugore literature, publications, or on our Website—such as "apparitions," "miracles," "messages," "visionaries," and similar—have the value of human witness and personal faith.

Nonetheless, in the waning months of 2013, as I was writing these pages, the American Bishops felt it necessary to remind readers through many media that no official endorsement of the experiences at Medjugore has been forthcoming. But we now have words to understand Baby Doe's visions; they have "the value of human witness and personal faith."[52]

In summary, there are very few approaches to discussions of these sorts of "visions." One approach, of course, dismisses them as symptoms of mental illnesses such as schizophrenia. If they are not seen as delusions, there may be explanations offered in mystical traditions. Baby Doe might have been lying, mistaken, or the recipient of spiritual favors from God. The Church does not condone any approach out of hand. Privately, I believe that if her visions brought her comfort, solace, encouragement, there is no harm in supposing they may have come from God. In any case, her visions are not proof of mental illness or of sainthood. They were personal to her and verified her religious belief in her own mind.

She recorded visions as nightly dream events in her life in far greater detail than the type of apparitions discussed above. In general, contemporary people do not regard dream visions as bizarre. Many people are fascinated by their dreams and keep journals to record them. The issue of whether they are external or internal becomes moot. For the Irish, the phenomenon known as a "dream-out" would have motivated Baby Doe to record her dreams in order to track how prophecy was functioning in her dream life. In this way, a dream sets up an expectation that subsequent events may bear out. Until such events confirm the prophetic nature of the dream, the expectation can function as a caution, a warning, a possible solution to a problem. One may profitably make decisions as a kind of wager that the dream is of this type. One can defend oneself against pending evils as appropriate.

The 5th century theorist Macrobius developed an analysis of dreams based on five types, and this wisdom was part of the common heritage of Western civilization until it was replaced by the theories of Sigmund Freud and Carl Jung in the twentieth century. Lizzie could have learned about it in literature class where dream visions constituted a major literary genre. Macrobius' typology included five types of dream: 1) the *somnium* presents an allegorical vision, prophesying the future via symbolic figures. This type of dream vision requires interpretation (one might say, in modern terms, literary exegesis). 2) the *visio* is a dream that comes true historically. The Irish tradition called this a "dream-out." Baby Doe wrote her daughter Silver about her dream that the number six shaft in the Matchless was flooding. Her subsequent letter verifies that it was indeed the number six that was causing all the trouble, "as I knew it would," she writes. 3) the *oraculum* is a prophetic vision mediated by authority such as an angel. Biblical dream visions are often of this type, as when Joseph is advised in a dream not to divorce his betrothed Mary. 4) A type of "misleading" dream is the *insomnium*, where dreams are invaded by bodily disturbances such as hunger or thirst. Sigmund Freud quite rightly amended this type to include psychological disturbances, desire, fear, guilt. In historical or prophetic terms, these dreams are "false," but they manifest a dreamer's psychic state and so are useful to psychoanalysts for understanding the dreamer. Many of Baby Doe's dreams manifest her earlier-life guilt, and these are what I term her "penitential" dreams.

5) Lastly, the *visium* involved nightmares with supernatural contact, a bad spirit called an incubus. There are reasons for Macrobius to reject this as a true dream as well, as it has no positive value as do the first three types. However, Baby Doe's visionary experiences appear to have included this type. Since fifteen hundred years of recorded tradition supported such experience of evil spirits, it is little wonder Lizzie recognized it in her own experience.

Baby Doe may not have been familiar with Macrobius or his medieval commentators such as Pascalis Romanus, but these ideas were part of the common knowledge of the culture, and dream visions had constituted an important literary genre for centuries. She definitely believed in dreams as prophetic, whether through allegorical figures or dream-outs. Baby Doe was especially interested in the pictures in her dreams, the allegorical figures. She drew, for example, a deer in moonlight, signed by E. Tabor, which was found in the cabin after Lizzie's death. This is certainly an example of Macrobius' *somnium*. Mrs. Tabor had identified this as one of her visions.[53] What meaning for Baby Doe this image had—how she interpreted the allegory—we do not know. What we can infer is that she used her visions to produce art—pictures or poems. Thus, we can grasp what she means when she calls them her "memoirs." Although many of these notations have survived, many have been lost as some of her large bags of such memoirs and notations were discarded after her death, and many disappeared when her cabin was ransacked after her death.

Baby Doe was, I surmise, still in the world of the Romantics like Samuel Taylor Coleridge who in 1816 published a beautiful poem describing the opulent world of Kubla Khan out of a vision which he well knew was induced by the opiate laudanum. If a dream vision is a source of Beauty, a scientific analysis of its sources in order to explain it away constitutes a form of desecration. Baby Doe's inner life was, I maintain, very much that of a nineteenth century Romantic. Sources were not important to her because she trusted her gift of discernment. After determining the source as good or evil, little else matters because God can work through any kind of natural or supernatural medium—dreams, apparitions, visions, (even drug-induced) in locutions—and in direct experience—to communicate with His people.

Why was she so focused on her dream life? How was her penitent personality connected to her visionary experience? Or was it? We are brought to a third aspect of her inner life beyond her status as the devout penitent and visionary. We come to terms, thirdly, with her well-known "persecution complex." Here is a further complication, but one that suggests her visionary and dream life in some cases offset for her a life often governed by fears.

By 1933, two years before her death, her mental problems may be divided into two categories: an onset of dementia traceable to the last two or three years of life, at age 78, until her death at age 81. Our investigations in the archives of the Sisters of Charity of Leavenworth yielded the memory that, the sisters recalled, in the last two years, Baby Doe was "losing it." A condition caused by hardening of the arteries feeding the brain may not be the same as "going mad next to Matchless"—imputed to Mrs. Tabor. There is something quite predictable about old-age dementia. Less commonly, she suffered, as everyone knew, from what was then called a "persecution complex."—in modern terminology, paranoid personality disorder.

According to the National Institute of Health, the World Health Organization, and other sites on the Internet, paranoid personality disorder is defined as: "a psychiatric state in which a person has a long-term distrust and suspicion of others but does not have a full blown psychotic disorder such as schizophrenia." The onset often occurs in early adulthood, is more common in men than women, and may involve genetic factors. Environmental factors "may play a role as well." These persons are often querulous, moody, somewhat narcissistic, and sensitive to criticism. From a list of symptoms on these sites we learn that such persons fear that others have hidden motives, feel in danger that others will exploit them, retreat into social isolation, harbor a hostile attitude, have difficulty working with others. Their highly suspicious nature leads to social isolation, and "they severely limit their social lives." Wikipedia adds that this "pervasive long-standing suspiciousness and generalized mistrust of others" leads sufferers to feel endangered and to "look for signs and threats of that danger, potentially not appreciating other evidence." The World Health Organization lists similar symptoms: excessive sensitivity to rebuffs, a tendency to bear grudges persistently, and difficulty forgiving injuries or slights. PPD sufferers distort experience by misconstruing the neutral or friendly actions of others as hostile or contemptuous.

Does the PPD shoe fit? A typical example is revealed in a story about how the citizens of Leadville saved Baby Doe's life one cold day. When no more mortgages were available, and the miners couldn't be paid, Baby Doe would attempt to run the machinery herself, donning work clothes and scampering up and down the ladder of the central mine shaft. We hear a fascinating account of her in the early years of the 1910 decade (presumably between managers T.M. Ramey and G.W. Casey). Leadville historian Edward Blair reported this incident, as told him in the 1970s by a Leadville businessman:

As you know, Baby Doe had been operating the mine by herself, negotiating the ladder on foot, up and down, several times each week. This was no mean feat for a woman in her late fifties and clearly she thought [of] some way to lessen the burden.

One morning, Leadville was startled to see huge clouds of smoke billowing from the stacks of the Matchless. Converging on the mine, they found that Baby Doe had put the engine and hoist back in working order, insofar as she was able from her limited knowledge of the subject. The fire, fueled by wood, had built up a head of steam in the boiler. And Baby Doe herself had rigged up an ingenious method of controlling the operation of the lift from either the top or the bottom of the shaft.

What Baby Doe did not know was the fact that the governor, which controlled the steam pressure, was rusted and frozen. When the crowd of curious Leadvillites arrived on the scene, pressure had built up to the point where an explosion was imminent. They blew the boilers by other means, banked the fire, and then dismantled enough of the device so that Baby Doe could not possibly repair the tank and repeat the operation.

Naturally, Baby Doe was furious, and regarded the operation as a plot against her. However, she was forced to return to her customary method of climbing up and down the long, steep ladder.

The teller of this account sums up: "The biographies of Baby Doe all seem to picture her as sitting around during her Leadville period after Tabor's death, mourning him and dreaming about the past. The records indicate that she was a far more realistic, resourceful woman."[54] She was also prone to regard the assistance of others as part of a plot against her. In a 1935 memoir about her in the

Denver Catholic Register, the reporter, after remarking on her upbeat conversation and "brilliant mind" says: "She told weird stories about attempts to wrest the Matchless mine, claiming that part of her property was burned or bombed a number of times."[55]

A further example of her paranoia can be inferred from her behavior during the winter of 1898 which she and Lillie spent in New York, seeking relief from certain health issues. There, she reported that she was being followed and that it was necessary to move her quarters rather often from one location to another. While this appears to be more evidence of paranoia, an odd occurrence also marked her stay in New York. An anonymous blackmailer wrote Horace Tabor in Denver that he had evidence of Baby Doe dancing the risqué can-can in a bistro. We are presented with a question: Which is more common—a beautiful woman walking in public being followed by curious men, or a beautiful woman imagining she is being followed? I vote for the former. I also think the beautiful woman being followed could be suffering from paranoid personality disorder.

The foregoing description of paranoid personality disorder is somewhat simplified and not endorsed by expert opinion regarding Baby Doe Tabor. Nonetheless, I find a description of a personality disorder convincing. Phrases like "somewhat narcissistic, pervasive, long-standing suspiciousness, generalized mistrust, self-chosen social isolation, expectation of exploitation by others" all resonate for anyone who has closely studied the life of Baby Doe Tabor. Her fierce defense of the Matchless mine before the onset of dementia reflects such a disposition. Furthermore, evidence suggests that her social isolation was operating by 1894 when her husband and two daughters dined in the public dining room of the Windsor Hotel while she kept to their rooms, not appearing in public. Even as early as 1882 when she was Tabor's mistress, she maintained her privacy, working on scrapbooks in their living quarters and only appearing heavily veiled in public with Horace in the year before they were married. As usual, ambiguity surrounds most of her behaviors and her reclusiveness in 1882 may have arisen from shame or even from her mourning the recent death of her and Harvey Doe's baby son.

But, as the saying goes, even paranoids have enemies, and discussion of paranoid personality disorder underscores caveats such as fear "without justification," "unsubstantiated grounds for suspicion." Did Baby Doe have grounds for her fearful, suspicious attitude? Far more, indeed, than any other celebrity in Colorado history. Negative publicity had followed her everywhere. In the mid-1880s, Eugene Field, with the power of the Denver press behind him, satirized the Tabor couple mercilessly, spreading libel in the name of humor. The scandal of the Washington wedding (March 1883), affected her deeply as it publicized the McCourt family's false witness. These, and the attribution of bigamy to Horace, based on the Durango divorce fiasco and the alleged St. Louis wedding in 1882, were only the beginning. Gossip about her adulterous relationship with Jake Sands buzzed throughout Denver. The multiple risks of being cheated in the mining industry assailed her as Horace's wife as well as his widow.[56] The list of names of those whom Horace had befriended, treated with generosity, set up in business, and who later cheated him, is so long as to be indecent. And, like all ultra-wealthy people, the Tabors had to worry about the safety of their children and defend them against kidnappers. One of the last deep insults came at a city-wide celebration in Denver of the movie premier in 1932, based on David Karsner's mean-spirited caricature of Horace, *Silver Dollar*. "That book and that movie broke my heart," she reported. It was, she said, "a pack of lies."

Such individual instances in Baby Doe's life, numbering in the thousands, help us understand how appropriate fear and suspicion can morph into baseless fear and suspicion, can throw a generally well-balanced woman into an imbalanced one as memory conflates the past with the present. Leadville residents in the 1930s did appreciate the background that led to Baby Doe's state as "odd, queer, tetched." It is almost as if those contributing environmental factors struck them as justifiable paranoia, her well-known and understandably predictable "persecution complex." As the *Denver Catholic Register* reporter stated, "There is no doubt that the scandals surrounding her marriage to Horace. . . somewhat imbalanced her." Helen Skala also noted: "The scandal surrounding her wedding in Washington had made a deep and lasting mark."[57]

We must recognize also that her paranoid personality could have flourished simply because of some genetic inheritance without the environmental provocations. This is one of those negative propositions that cannot be proved. It is a mysterious nature-nurture question. However, her daughter Lillie seems also to have been a reclusive personality. When reporters visited her at home upon the occasion of Silver's death in 1925 and again when her mother passed on ten years later, Lillie opened the door just a crack and refused to be interviewed. In 1935 she denied being Baby Doe's daughter, saying she was a niece. Neighbors told the reporters they rarely saw her. And, the fact that she married a cousin suggests that her social circle outside her Midwestern McCourt family was not a large one. The evidence is slim but suggestive.

When we put Lizzie's behavior into a perspective where evidence supports what passes for normal rather than "tetched" or bizarre, there is a great deal of this. When she walked into Leadville, she liked to discuss the latest mining technology with the inspectors, and this she did with clarity of mind. When visitors came unexpectedly to her "shrine" at the Matchless, she may have pointed a rifle at them, but she also assessed their intentions and judged whether they were potentially harmful or not. Recall how she decided Frank Waters' sister Naomi had a good heart like her Mr. Tabor and how she welcomed the Iacino's because they asked for an invitation in advance of their visit. Her fear caused her to prevent the teenage Silver Dollar from entering the homes of anyone she did not know, but according to Mrs. Struthman, Baby Doe relented at her daughter's pleadings, and gave her permission. She was guarded and her guardianship sometimes exceeded reasonable bounds. Her protectiveness of her grown daughter Silver was experienced as an over-protectiveness and a disrespect of Silver's right, at 25 years old, to shape her own future. When Silver fell into a life of alcoholism and drug dependency in Chicago, Lizzie cried out appropriately, "Oh, my dear Silver, she has lost her mind." When she recognized that visitors on Fryer Hill were children, she put aside her gun and smiled benignly or gave them a friendly wave. Invited or expected guests were welcomed and accorded hospitality. Newsmen were shunned; she had always despised publicity, as she wrote in a letter to her brother Peter McCourt. Indeed, in this she conformed to the social standard and cultural norm of that time, during which the seeking of publicity reeked of bad taste if not moral degeneracy.

The imputation of derangement bothered her brother Phil McCourt, who, in an interview shortly after her death, lamented her reputation as a "madwoman." Phil was aging, and at 78 his health was failing. He wept for his sister. "'I loved her better than anyone in the world', he said. 'She was a splendid woman. You see, I knew that. I lived with her in the cabin [for four months in 1932] and we worked on the mine together. Don't let them say she was foolish, or had wild ideas.'"[58] The *Denver Catholic Register's* news story also touched on this issue: "But one could talk to her at that time [1927] for hours and be convinced that she was sagacious enough to manage her business affairs, despite the rumor that she was somewhat unbalanced."[59]

Another reason to re-evaluate our opinion of her mental imbalance rests on the Catholic teachings about discernment. Recall that Lizzie's middle name was "Bonduel," the Jesuit missionary in Wisconsin who was a close friend of the McCourt family. Moreover, Fr. Guida, who had been a spiritual advisor to the Tabors at Sacred Heart parish, was a Jesuit. Jesuit founder, St. Ignatius of Loyola, had a great deal to say about "discernment of spirits." This power is one of the gifts of the Holy Spirit—a charisma. (1 Cor 12:10) It means that a person can distinguish the moral disposition of souls for good or evil. Mystics like St. Teresa of Avila encountered spirits sometimes without reassurance as to who was which. When she sought counsel from her spiritual advisors, she received mixed messages: some suggested she could depend on her intuition of good spirits and some doubted, assuming that Satan was not to be ruled out as a source. Teresa experienced great anguish because of this. Lizzie, on the other hand, believed in her ability to discern. When near the Matchless she "saw Papa"—Horace—she knew he was good, a benefactor. When she observed the outward demeanor of people she met, she inferred their goodness or their badness from their appearance. (See her cautious assessment of Frank Waters' sister Naomi described above.) The calendar notation just before her death that she "saw three devils" says she spoke to them, and perhaps she banished them. All these examples support her implied claim to have received a gift, a power, of discernment. When we envision her, shotgun in hand, persecution complex part of her history, we should recall this other motivation, a reasonable process of assessing whether visitors are friend or foe—her power of discernment. On the surface, the reasonable assessment and the paranoia appear much the same.

Her personality disorder precluded a full-blown psychotic disorder. But consistent with a personality disorder, there is something exaggerated about her defensiveness, suspicion, reclusiveness. She *did* hold grudges, even against her once-beloved brother Peter because he intervened on behalf of her daughters from their experience of the tyranny of Baby Doe's fear and over-protectiveness. She never forgave those who cheated Horace as his empire finally disintegrated in 1896. All in all, her mental problems appear as paranoid *moods* pervasive when she defended the property near her cabin, had to share power over the Matchless profits, should they succeed, and as encroaching when time lapses threw her back on her solitude and as her solitude invited fantasies evoked out of sense deprivation.

Her interest in prophetic dreams, allegories and dream-outs, presupposes her fears. She used dreams to reassure herself about the future, or to discern possible dangers. When she envisioned Silver riding on a golden horse, she was reassured. When she saw a dragon in her coffee grounds, she waited and, surely enough, four days later she reported something terrible had happened. To others, reading tea leaves, she was able to offer cautions. Insofar as such visions set her mind at rest by rendering auspicious results, her dreams could function as a defense against her fears, prove her suspicions groundless, and mitigate her paranoia.

Sometimes her dreams are "penitential," referring to guilty feelings such as the incident caused when Maggie McCourt's husband, Wm Courtney kissed her passionately at the wedding reception and caused a family uproar. Baby Doe was only a teenager at that time, but she bore the burden of family criticism, her having spoiled the happy occasion of her sister's wedding. Fifty years later, she would still be dreaming that Courtney kissed her. Furthermore, it was her Washington wedding that compromised her father's integrity and cost him a happy death. The *Denver Catholic Register's* writer knew this: "There is no doubt that her sufferings in late years when she lived in a shack on a bleak hillside at Leadville, close to the famous mine, somewhat undermined her reason."[60] This desire for assurance also explains the existence of the ouija board in her cabin after she died. She recorded dreams where her family stood in silent judgment of her and she was reduced to humble and abject states.

Thus we have been presented with issues about her sanity, especially because of her legendary state as "going mad next to Matchless." We have seen that paranoia governed her moods in certain contexts and that many of the symptoms of paranoid personality disorder apply. We have seen that imbalances are offset by her presentation of herself as even-tempered, clear-minded, and that she habitually discerned between those who did not threaten her, such as children, and those who might truly threaten her such as "lyin' thievin'" newspaper reporters invading her property. We have acknowledged that her pervasive suspicion of anyone who wanted to lease or work the Matchless revealed an imbalance in her thinking. Even when she sought financial help from friends at the *Denver Catholic Register,* she would, after a time for consideration, withdraw into her fears and cut off communications. There was the story about a Thanksgiving dinner to which she was invited by a Leadville resident, an invitation she declined. But she showed up to participate in the dinner because she believed that she was safe from harm if her presence was unexpected. (O'Brien, 5). She seems to have inhabited a bi-level world, half normal, half paranoid.

What is fascinating about her in view of her imbalances is the question of her visions and supernatural encounters. Are these to be understood, if at all, as symptoms of her psychological disease? Are these authentic visions? Was she, as some in Leadville surmised, a saint? Can we answer these questions? Perhaps the legend so well documented in many biographies and the facts about her life that I have presented here form a Gordian knot, an insoluble conundrum. And if her life is a mystery defying reduction into rational explanation, what does that mean for those of us who write and read about her with interest and perhaps fascination? Are our own lives an open book or do we share in the mystery of what, as inner persons, we remain—defying explanation?

Epilogue

In late winter, 1935, a man passing through Leadville stopped to give an old woman a lift. She accepted and asked him to buy her a bottle of whiskey, which he did. His passenger, he was amazed to find, was Baby Doe Tabor. He had the honor of a photo op with her. Together they shared a drink, Lizzie sipping from her tin cup. "Medicine," she commented wryly. Within a month or two, she was gone. Ruefully, he reflected on the cheap whiskey he had provided her. Would it have been too much for him to have offered the Silver Queen of the West a decent brand of her last bottle of whiskey?

On March 7, 1935, Baby Doe Tabor, more matchless than the mine she cherished, was discovered dead of a heart attack (not, as first reported, frozen to death). She had fallen on her back, her arms flung out in the shape of a cross. This fact was not lost on those who had known her well. There were those who considered her a saint because of her absorption in prayer and other-worldly encounters. She would surely have scoffed at the idea. There were those, too, who recalled only the sinner.

Her body had been discovered by her neighbor Sue Bonnie and Sue's friend Tom French, who lived in a nearby cabin. Since the last notation on her wall calendar had been dated February 22, 1935, it was assumed she had died not long after that date. Nor had her neighbors seen anything from her smokestack for several days.

Lizzie's brother Willard hastened to Leadville to represent the family, the only McCourt to do so. After some discussion, it was decided that her funeral would be held in Leadville. Thus, at the Church of the Annunciation, Father Horgan, voice tinged with an Irish brogue, addressed the crowded church in a brief ceremony. "We pray for the remission of any sin for which she may have deserved punishment. . . .We pray she will go to everlasting rest. Deliver her not into the hands of her enemies but let her be taken to Paradise."[61] No eulogy, no judgments, no condemnation.

Following the funeral mass, her body was carried by train to Denver to Mt. Olivet cemetery (Mt. Olivet was the place from which Jesus ascended into heaven) to be interred with the remains of her beloved Horace and a brother, Stephen McCourt. Today, the impressive marker, donated by wealthy admirers, is a stopping place for those touring the historic cemetery.

Meanwhile, in Leadville, Baby Doe's cabin was ransacked, allegedly by youths looking for a stash of silver which never existed. Her purse contained merely a couple of dollars and change—leading to reports that that was all she had. This figure was soon revised to report an amount of $227.65. Reports of her impoverishment, however, turned out to be exaggerated once her many trunks which had languished unattended in Denver and Leadville were opened, revealing, the next estimate said, around $650.00. In the final analysis, her estate contained over 12,500 items of historic interest and left-over belongings, once-expensive, from the glory days. Enough, as one reporter noted, to have eased her later years. Indeed! Today, just about any item—a glove, a letter, a photo—is collectible and so has a market value.

The next issue: Who who will inherit Baby Doe's estate? Lillie Tabor Last of Milwaukee, now Lizzie's only living daughter, did not claim her inheritance. In fact, she told reporters that she was the daughter of Horace's brother John Tabor. The 1930 census reveals that she then listed her place of birth as California. She had, in effect, divorced herself from a relationship to Baby Doe. Since no one in the McCourt family claimed the inheritance, it was entrusted to the Colorado Historical Society and the care of Edgar McMechen. For nearly fifteen years, her papers were held privately until McMechen's death in the late 1940s.

Interest in Baby Doe might have subsided after her death, except that historian Carolyn Bancroft planned to write about her. Her efforts to research the biography were thwarted, however. In 1937, just two years after Baby Doe's death, Bancroft received $3,000 from *True Story Magazine* to produce a five-part series on the legendary Baby Doe. Since the story for the confessions magazine had to be presented in first person, Bancroft agreed to find a source who had known Baby Doe. After much difficulty, she accomplished interviews with Sue Bonnie, who agreed to be represented as the narrator of the series. In addition, Bancroft looked eagerly to Edgar McMechen, curator of the Colorado Historical Society Museum but was refused access to the Tabor collection. The result was a much romanticized, fictionalized story. Bancroft's 80-page biography of the 1950s, *Silver Queen: The Fabulous Story of Baby Doe Tabor,* maintained the fictions, according to historian Duane Smith. After an initial denial about the *True Story* authorship, she "eventually confessed to having written the Bonnie stories. . . . She described her *Silver Queen* as 'never pretending to be anything but a fictionalized story.'" He notes that Bancroft's high reputation as a historian meant that "others accepted her writings and facts as gospel."[62]

Subsequent biographies suffered, then, from tainted sources, and the legend departed from the reality of Baby Doe Tabor. Bancroft's Baby Doe is a secular figure, with no apparent ethnic identity. She is pathetically tossed about in her stormy life, never in charge of her own fate. The implication is that she agonizes over her lost fortune and longs to realize her hopes for restored riches. This materialistic Baby Doe is also falsely placed in a "love triangle" and is pictured as a rival to Augusta Tabor. The 1957 opera, *The Ballad of Baby Doe,* dramatized and set to music all these misconceptions. Bancroft's Baby Doe has no religion and no regret over her sexual transgressions. Rather, the exaggeration of her non-conformist spirit left the impression that she cared little for respectability (like Bancroft herself).

However, she was, in fact, an absolute icon for Family. She could not abide signs of disloyalty, especially from Uncle Pete, and she could not understand that what was good for her daughters might be different from what was good for her or what she judged was best for them might be too influenced by her *ideal* of Family. Since her family was nearly the exclusive focus of her life, she naturally expected loyalty and sacrifice from her siblings. Of course, these were assessed on her terms. Thus, when her younger brother Pete thwarted her need to keep her daughters near her, Baby Doe was furious with him.

The great tragedy of her life was witnessing the "down and out" of Silver's life trajectory. In what appears as a truly Classical style tragedy, where one's errors of judgment result in one's downfall or failure, we see Lizzie's failure as a mother caused to some degree by her attempts to keep Silver as her child, her baby. That Silver might have suffered a similar fate even if her mother had let her adult child pursue her own fate (married in Leadville to Ed Brown, for example), we cannot know. What matters are the facts of the case. Lizzie refused to listen to reason concerning her daughter's plans to marry in Colorado and so she drove her away to suffer from her own addictive and self-destructive behavior.

As to her visitations by angels and devils, we can only acknowledge that such were the givens of her experience. These she notated only in the last year and half of her life. Any attempts we may make to explain these away as religious nonsense or mental illness lead us to dead ends. We do not know what caused her visionary life. And if we did know, it would not matter. These were private and personal spiritual experiences. Their meaning is constituted by what they meant to her. We need not intrude upon them with sophisticated guesses or scientific prejudices.

Many have quoted the motto on the curtain of the Tabor Grand Opera House as though it fit Baby Doe's life to a "T.": "So fleet the works of men, back to the earth again/ Ancient and holy things fade like a dream." It sounds so utterly grand! However, Baby Doe would have agreed with the first line but probably not the second. Ancient and holy things had not faded but had become more important.

Baby Doe is remembered for many virtues: loyalty to family and Faith, perseverance, self-sacrifice, modesty, piety, value on historical preservation. Her sheer pluck in the face of adversity is astounding. She never whined or indulged in self pity. On the contrary, she was grateful to God, notably, as she said, that He gave her a strong back to bear whatever tribulations life sent her way. Whether because of the legend—her symbolic importance as a representative of the Gilded Age, the Gay '90s, and the "boom and bust" of American economics—or because of her indomitable spirit—she has become not only a figure admired—though once despised—but one now remembered often with great affection and esteem.

Bibliography

Archives of the Sisters of Charity of Leavenworth KS, private correspondence.

Arp, Louisa Ward. *Denver in Slices.* Denver, CO: Sage Books, 1959.

Bancroft, Carolyn. *Augusta Tabor: Her Side of the Scandal.* Boulder, CO: Johnson Publishing Co., 1955.

______. "Belle of Oshkosh" in *Denver Westerners Brand Book.* IX, 1955. 115-130.

______. *The Brown Palace in Denver: Hotel of Plush, Power and Presidents.* Boulder, CO: Johnson Publishing Co., 1980.

______. *Gulch of Gold.* Denver, CO: Sage Books, 1955.

______. *Silver Queen: The Fabulous Story of Baby Doe Tabor.* Boulder, CO: Johnson Books, 2000 [1955].

______. *Tabor's Matchless Mine and Lusty Leadville.* Boulder, CO: Johnson Publishing Co., 1984.

Barrett, Marjorie. "Memories of Baby Doe Tabor." *Rocky Mountain News,* March 10, 1968, 7.

Blair, Edward and E. Richard Churchill. *Everybody Came to Leadville.* Gunnison, CO: Timberline Books, 1971.

Blair, Edward. *Leadville: Colorado's Magic City.* Boulder, CO: Pruett Publishing Co., 1980.

_____. *Tabor Family Album*. Leadville, CO: Timberline Books, 1981 [1974].

Buchanan, John and Doris. *A Story of the Fabulous Windsor Hotel.* Denver, CO: The A.B. Hirschfeld Press, 1956

Brown, Slater. *The Heyday of Spiritualism*. New York, NY: Pocket Book Edition, 1972. [Hawthorne, 1970].

Bueler, Gladys R. *Colorado's Colorful Characters.* Boulder, CO: Pruett Publishing Co., 1981.

Burke, John. *The Legend of Baby Doe: The Colorful Life and Times of the Silver Queen of the West.* New York, NY: G.P. Putnam's Sons, 1974.

Coquoz Rene L. *King Pleasure Reigned in 1896: The Story of the Fabulous Leadville Ice Palace.* Boulder, CO: Johnson Publishing Company, 1969.

_____. *The Leadville Story: Brief History 1860-1960.* Boulder, CO: Johnson Publishing Co., 1971.

_____. *Tales of Early Leadville, Part Three* (3-part series). Boulder, CO: Johnson Books, 1976. Part Two published 1964 by Johnson Books. Part One published in Leadville, CO by Rene L. Coquoz Books, 1961.

Dorsey, Anna H. *The Old Gray Rosary: Refuge of Sinners.* New York: P. O'Shea Publishers, 1899.

Erskine, Helen. *Out of This World: A Collection of Hermits and Recluses.* New York, NY: G.P. Putnam's Sons, 1953.

Fallis, Edwina. *When Denver and I Were Young.* Denver, CO: Big Mountain Press, 1956.

Furman, Evelyn E. *Silver Dollar Tabor: A Leaf in the Storm.* Aurora, CO: The National Writers Press, 1982.

_____. *The Tabor Opera House.* Leadville, CO: privately published, 1972.

Gandy, Lewis. *The Tabors: A Footnote to Western History.* New York, NY: Press of the Pioneers, Inc., 1934.

Griswold, Don and Jean Harvey Griswold. *History of Leadville and Lake County, Colorado: From Mountain Solitude to Metropolis.* 2 vols. Denver, CO: Colorado Historical Society and the University Press of Colorado, 1996.

Hall, Gordon Langley. *The Two Lives of Baby Doe*. Philadelphia, PA: Macrae Smith Co., 1962.

_____. "History of Oshkosh." Archives, Oshkosh Public Library Oshkosh, WI. (1895). Description of a flash fire reprinted from the newspaper, *Oshkosh Daily Northwestern,* mid 1870s.

Karsner, David. *Silver Dollar*. New York, NY: Crown Publishing, 1958 [1932].

McMechen, Edgar C. *The Tabor Story*. Denver, CO: Colorado Historical Society,

Mehaffey, Karen Rae. *The Afterlife: Mourning Rituals and the Mid-Victorians*. Pipestone, MN: Laser Writers Publishing, 1993.

Moynihan, Betty. *Augusta Tabor: A Pioneering Woman*. Evergreen, CO: Cordillera Press, 1988.

Noel, Thomas J. *The City and the Saloon: Denver 1858-1916*. Niwot, CO: Colorado UP, 1996 [Nebraska UP 1982].

O'Brien, Teresa. *The Bitter Days of Baby Doe Tabor and Memories of the High Country*. Leadville, CO: self-published, 1963.

Parkhill, Forbes. "How Tabor Lost His Millions." In *Denver Westerner's Brand Books,* IX 1953. 133-148.

Radetsky, Ralph. "Brother Weeps and Is Proud of Baby Doe Tabor." The *Denver Post,* March 18, 1935.

Riley, Marilyn Griggs. "Sin, Gin, and Jasmine: The Controversial Career of Caroline Bancroft. *Colorado Heritage Magazine*. Denver, CO: Colorado Historical Society, (Spring) 2002. 31-46.

Roberts, Martha Gaby. *Honeymaid: The Story of Silver Dollar Tabor*. Denver, CO: Golden Bell Press, 1977. (Fictionalized account based on in-depth research.)

Skala, Helen, et. al. *Tales from the Old Timers*. Leadville, CO: self-published, 1972. See "The Last Years of Baby Doe Tabor" among three articles included in this collection.

Smith, Duane. *Horace Tabor: His Life and the Legend*. Niwot, CO: Colorado UP, 1989.

Struthman, Mattie. "High Country Memories." *Colorado Magazine.* Vol 29:1 (Winter) 1952. 33-37.

Temple, Judith Nolte. *Baby Doe Tabor: The Madwoman in the Cabin.* Norman, OK: Oklahoma UP, 2007.

_____. "The Demons of Elizabeth Tabor: Mining Dreams and Visions from the Matchless." *Colorado Heritage.* Denver, CO: Colorado Historical Society, (Winter) 2001. 3-21.

Thomas, Sewell. *Silhouettes of Charles S. Thomas: Colorado Governor and United States Senator.* Caldwell, ID: The Caxton Press, 1959.

Tomashek, Peter. "Monument to Penance." Newsclip, July 23, 1953. Tabor collection, Stephen Hart Library, Colorado Historical Society, Denver, CO.

Varnell, Jeanne. *Women of Consequence: The Colorado Women's Hall of Fame.* Boulder, CO: Johnson Books, 1999.

Vernon, John. *All For Love.* New York, NY: Simon & Shuster, 1995.

Walsh, Michael, ed. *Butler's Lives of the Saints.* San Francisco, CA: Harper Collins, 1991. First published 1756-1759 and updated through many editions.

Waters, Frank. *The Colorado.* Athens, OH: Swallow Press, Ohio UP, 1985 [1946].

Williston, George. *Here They Dug the Gold.* New York: Reynal & Hitchcock, 1946.

Notes

[1] Father Bonduel was a celebrity in what was then the "northwestern" territory of the U.S., Wisconsin and Illinois. He is remembered as the first pastor of St. Peter's Catholic parish of Oshkosh although he was a visiting priest and not a resident one. Since Peter McCourt Sr. was a founding member of the parish, he was proud to have the celebrated Jesuit say mass in his home or in McCourt Hall before the church structure was complete. Some sources say Lizzie chose the Bonduel name as her own middle one, and others believe it was given to her at baptism, or shortly thereafter. See *Florimand J. Bonduel: Missionary to Wisconsin Territory* by Malcolm Rosholt and John Britten Gehl. Amherst, WI: Palmer Publications, Inc., 1976.

[2] John Burke, *The Legend of Baby Doe: The Colorful Life and Times of the Silver Queen of the West,* New York, NY: G.P. Putnam's Sons, 1974, 12.

[3] Reprint from the *Oshkosh Daily Northwestern,* 1875 in *A History of the City of Oshkosh, 1895.* Archives, Oshkosh Public Library, Oshkosh, WI.

[4] *Ibid.*

[5] Charles Nevitt, personal scrapbook, Archives, Oshkosh Public Museum, Oshkosh, WI, 31.

[6] Personal correspondence from Bob McCabe, Lizzie's nephew, to historian Edward Blair, Archives, Lake County Public Library, Leadville, CO.

[7] Varnell, Jeanne, *Women of Consequence:The Colorado Women's Hall of Fame,* Boulder, CO:, Johnson Publishing Company, 1999, xxx.

[8] Carolyn Bancroft, "Belle of Oshkosh," *Denver Westerners Roundup,* Denver Westerners Corral, Denver, CO, 115.

[9] According to a letter archived at the Lake County Public Library in Leadville, CO, a writer who wished to remain anonymous claimed that "it was well known," at least in the mountain towns, that Harvey Doe was sowing wild oats in Denver, womanizing and sometimes drinking excessively. This lends credence to Lizzie's claim that she had been abandoned in Central City. It should be added, however, that Harvey Doe returned to the Midwest after his divorce from Lizzie, married a widow with a child, engaged in a cigar business, and apparently lived a respectable life in a long-lasting marriage.

[10] *Ibid.*

[11] Helen Erskine, *Out of This World: A Collection of Hermits and Recluses,* New York, NY: G.P. Putnam's Sons, 1953, 292-293.

[12] Edwina Fallis, *When Denver and I Were Young,* Denver, CO: Big Mountain Press, 1956, 87-88.

[13] James Harvey, "Recollections of the Early Theatre," *Colorado Magazine,* September, 1940, Vol. 17:5, 166.

[14] Duane Smith, *Horace Tabor: Life and Legend,* Niwot, CO: Colorado UP, 1989, xi.

[15] Burke, *op cit.,* 98-103. Burke presents a fascinating summary of the complications resulting from Augusta's various maneuvers which exasperated Horace, who had been given to believe Augusta would cooperate in an uncontested divorce only to be constantly thwarted.

[16] Private correspondence, archives, Lake County Public Library, Leadville, CO.

[17] *Oshkosh Daily Northwestern* n.d. Clipping file, Archives, Tabor Collection, Oshkosh Public Museum, Oshkosh, WI.

[18] *Ibid.*

[19] Molly Brown, the unsinkable, was also a member of Sacred Heart parish. Using this Catholic connection, she introduced a friend known only as B.Z.to Baby Doe on at least one occasion. See Marjorie Barrett, "Memories of Baby Doe Tabor," *Rocky Mountain News,* March 10, 1968, 7.

[20] ______. "Gene Field Blamed for Many Tabor Legends." *Leadville Herald Democrat,* February 2, 1935. Archives, Tabor file, newsclip, Western History Department, Denver Public Library, Denver, CO. Tabor biographer Lewis Cass Gandy provided the information herein.

[21] Lee Casey, "The Real Tabor" in the *Leadville Herald Democrat,* reprinted in Griswold & Griswold, *The History of Leadville and Lake County,* Denver, CO: Colorado Historical Society, 1986, Vol 2, 116:239.

[22] Synthesized from correspondence, Tabor collection, Stephen Hart Library, Calendar FF 173 #5, Colorado Historical Society, Denver CO.

[23] Mattie Edwards Struthman, "High Altitude Memories," *Colorado Magazine,* January, 1952, Vol 29:1 (Winter), 35.

[24] Evelyn Furman, *Silver Dollar Tabor: A Leaf in the Storm,* Aurora, CO: The National Writer's Press, 1982, 246.

[25] Judith Nolte Temple, *Baby Doe Tabor: The Madwoman in the Cabin.* Norman, OK: Oklahoma UP, 2007.

[26] "'Baby Doe' Tabor Leaves Religious Articles to Nun," newsclip of April 2, 1935. Archives, Chapter House, Sisters of Charity of Leavenworth, Leavenworth, KS.

[27] Griswold, Don and Jean Harvey Griswold. *History of Leadville and Lake County, Colorado: From Mountain Solitude to Metropolis.* Vol. I, Denver, CO: Colorado Historical Society and the University Press of Colorado, 1996.

[28] Ralph Radetsky, "Brother Weeps and Is Proud of Baby Doe Tabor," *Denver Post,* March 10, 1935. See files, Tabor collection, Western History Department, Denver Public Library, Denver, CO.

[29] Griswold, *op cit.* vol I, 2224.

[30] *Ibid.*

[31] Many pioneers chose gunny sacking for winter footwear. Fans of Baby Doe donated galoshes, but she declined to wear these emblems of unwelcome charity.

[32] Peter Tomashek, "Monument to Penance," newsclip dated July 23, 1953 in Tabor collection, Stephen Hart Library, Colorado Historical Society, Denver, CO.

[33] "Baby Doe Spent Last Years as Catholic," *Denver Catholic Register.* Newsclip, June 18, 1953. Tabor file, Western History Department. Denver Public Library, Denver, CO.

34 Letter to U.S. Representative Longworth, Archives, Colorado Historical Society, MSS 614, Box 10, FF#791, Stephen Hart Library, Denver, CO.

35 Teresa O'Brien, *The Bitter Days of Baby Doe Tabor and Memories of the High Country,* Leadville, CO: self-published, 1963, 5.

36 Griswold, *op cit.* vol I, 2224.

37 Xerox copy sent to the author from the archives of the Sisters of Charity of Leavenworth, KS, with the handwritten description: "Taken from Baby Doe's trunk in 1935. The trunk was left at St. Vincent's Hospital in Leadville until her death."

38 Marjorie Barrett, "Memories of Baby Doe Tabor," *Rocky Mountain News,* March 10, 1968, 7. See archives, Stephen Hart Library, Colorado Historical Society (History Colorado), Denver, CO.

39 Rene L. Coquoz, *The Saga of H.A.W. Tabor,* Boulder,CO: Johnson Publishing Co., 1978 [1973], 31-32.

40 *Ibid.,* 37.

41 Anna H. Dorsey, *The Old Gray Rosary: Refuge of Sinners,* NY: P. O'Shea Publisher, 1899, 13-14.

42 Helen Skala, et. al. *Tales From the Old Timers,* Leadville, CO: self-published, 1972, 13.

43 *Ibid.,* 10.

44 Frank Waters, *The Colorado,* Athens, OH: The Swallow Press, Ohio UP, 1985 27-29.

45 Marjorie Barrett, *op cit.*

46 Bancroft's search for Baby Doe artifacts, newsclip in *Denver Catholic Register,* Archives, Tabor Collection, Western History Department, Denver Public Library, Denver, CO.

47 Michael Walsh, ed., *Butler's Lives of the Saints,* rev. ed. New York, NY: HarperCollins, 1991, 335.

48 _____. Mrs. Tabor Often Called At Office of The Register," *Denver Catholic Register,* April 3, 1935, Tabor Collection, Western History Department, Denver Public Library, Denver, CO.

⁴⁹ Tabor clipping file, Western History Department, Denver Public Library, Denver, CO. Newsclip, no date.

⁵⁰ O'Brien, 6.

⁵¹ *Ibid.*, 5.

⁵² www.ourladycalls.com.

⁵³ O'Brien, 6.

⁵⁴ Donald H. Menzel, Personal correspondence to Edward Blair, April 25, 1973, Archives, Lake County Public Library, Leadville, CO.

⁵⁵ _____."Mrs. Tabor Often Called At Office of the Register, *op cit.* April 4, 1935.

⁵⁶ Risks included tunneling salting, digging horizontally under a neighbor's claim. See text p. 75.

⁵⁷ Skala, 12.

⁵⁸ Ralph Radetsky, "Brother Weeps and Is Proud of Baby Doe Tabor," *Denver Post,* March 10, 1935. Archives, Tabor collection, Western History Department, Denver Public Library, Denver, CO.

⁵⁹ "Mrs. Tabor Often Called at Office of the Register", *op cit. Denver Catholic Register,* April 4, 1935.

⁶⁰ *Ibid.*

⁶¹ _____. "Brief Rites for Baby Doe at Leadville," The *Sterling Advocate*, March 13, 1935. Tabor files, Western History Department, Denver Public Library, Denver CO.

⁶² Duane Smith, "Introduction," in T*he Legend of Baby Doe: The Life and Times of the Silver Queen of the West* by John Burke, [Richard O'Connor] Lincoln, NE: Nebraska UP, 1989 [1974].

Acknowledgements

I am grateful to the helpful staff at the following institutions: The Oshkosh Public Museum, Oshkosh, Wisconsin; the Stephen Hart Library, Colorado Historical Society, Denver, Colorado; the Western History Department, Denver Public Library, Denver, Colorado; the Lake County Public Library, Leadville, Colorado; the National Mining Museum, Leadville, Colorado. Their generous cooperation made this book possible. I am also grateful to the Sisters of Charity, Leavenworth, Kansas, Susan Hoskinson, and other individuals whose assistance and suggestions kept me focused throughout the development of the manuscript. Finally, research assistance from Darrell and Sandy Schulte provided an invaluable contribution to this book.

Printed in the USA
CPSIA information can be obtained
at www.ICGtesting.com
CBHW080952260924
R15629900002B/R156299PG13938CBX00162B/45